servants
of all

chiara lubich

servants of all

new city press, new york

Published in the United States by New City Press
the Publishing House of the Focolare Movement, Inc.
206 Skillman Avenue, Brooklyn, N.Y. 11211
©1978 by Citta Nuova Editrice, Rome, Italy
Translated from the original Italian edition
Uomini al Servizio di Tutti
by Hugh J. Moran
Printed by Wing Tai Cheung Printing Co., Hong Kong
Library of Congress Catalog Number: 78-59470
ISBN 0-911782-05-2

Nihil Obstat: Rev. Martin S. Rushford
                  Diocesan Censor
Imprimatur: Francis J. Mugavero, D.D.
                  Bishop of Brooklyn
Brooklyn, N.Y. May 19, 1978

FOREWORD

It is not an easy task to write the foreward to a book by Chiara Lubich, but it is certainly gratifying. Indeed, it is an opportunity I welcome and a source of personal consolation to be able to present these pages of theology and spirituality, which have been prepared with great care and dedication by someone who, with faith and love, has first tried to live what she has written.

Those who view the institutional Church only as a burden or a hindrance, and have therefore adopted the destructive attitude of mere protest, or have chosen the tortuous route of abandoning the Church, may regard any discussion of the hierarchy as outdated. But all who are seeking with a sincere heart to know Christ's Church better and to live its life more fully, will certainly find Chiara's presentation thoroughly relevant, and will read it with great profit. For without the hierarchy, the Church cannot exist, now or in the future, just as it is impossible - since divine Providence has decreed it otherwise - to think of Jesus without his Church.

It is difficult to know what to highlight in these various chapters, which together constitute a harmonious and unified whole. I could draw attention to the theological content; to the precise use of language; to the warmth and liveliness of Chiara's presentation; or to her love for the Church, which gently makes its presence felt in every word she writes. For if it is true that only the heart can enable us to see certain things, here we encounter someone whose heart is on fire, who succeeds in combining study and research with a profound experience of God, whom she has known and loved, especially through the Word and the Eucharist. And as we are well aware, true knowledge of God in the biblical sense lies well beyond any notions acquired through mere study and reasoning.

A careful reading of the various topics will immediately reveal that Chiara's approach is neither superficial nor dull, but profound and alive. Without getting lost in controversial theological issues - which, however, she does not overlook - the author goes straight to the heart of the matter, supported by the Scriptures, the Fathers of the Church, the Tradition of the Church, the documents of the Council, and the pronouncements of the Pope. As in all her other works, Chiara's reflections here reveal a great love for God; filial submission to his will; and an ardent desire to adhere fully to the divine plan of salvation, marvelously summed up in the incarnation of the Word, who desired to perpetuate his living presence among us in the Church he instituted.

This loving presence of Jesus in the Church as a whole and in its ministers - which is presented as a reflection of the life of the Trinity, an extension of heaven's life on earth - is a dominant theme which pervades the book, giving it a distinctive quality. Without this faith in the living presence of Christ in his Church, it would be pointless to speak about the hierarchy, which is the visible sign in the Church of the invisible presence of its Founder, Cornerstone and Head.

Another recurring theme is the classical idea that a Christian should strive to be of one mind with the Church. For Chiara, this is not a theory but a way of life. From the very beginning of the Focolare Movement, her attitude toward the hierarchy has been a living demonstration of this permanent readiness to think, to feel and to live at one with the Church, in respectful and spontaneous submission to the hierarchy, whom she has always obeyed - even in moments of painful misunderstandings and agonizing trials.

What Chiara has written here is an expression of her love and passion for the Church, and should not be understood simply as a literary exercise or an attempt to pursue mere theological disputation. It is intended as a service to truth, to enable us to view the hierarchy not as an oppressive power, but as a liberating instrument of service and a constructive force of love. If the book is read and meditated upon with this spirit, it will not be quickly forgotten as just another fleeting object of our attention, but its message will remain as a constant reminder to be put into practice in everyday life. Moreover, it will help us to have a greater love for the Church, and to see in it the presence of Jesus, alive in every member, and present within the community, especially in the hierarchy united with the Pope, who is the principle of unity of the college of bishops as well as of the whole Church.

The present volume, small in size but great in content, should not be read with the superficial curiosity of a hurried tourist, but rather with the attitude of a person who is seriously searching for the truth that can enlighten one's mind, inflame one's heart, and bring one to the fullness of life. And that is what I wish with all my heart to you, the fortunate readers, to whom this book is destined to bring a new love for that gift of God which comes to us through the hierarchy, the humble servant of humanity as it journeys toward the Father's house.

† Federico Didonet
Bishop of Rio Grande,
Brasil

CONTENTS

1.

The Rock

The unbelieving, often atheistic world in which we live claims to admire Jesus, just as many other ages in the past have done — each for its own reasons and in its own way. Though considered perhaps as merely human, he is esteemed — if for no other reason, than because he is an exceptional, unusual and fascinating figure. In fact, because of the great interest he inspires in the artistic world, and the popularity of artistic productions dealing with him, many say that Jesus is now back in fashion.

Nevertheless it is evident that today's world is caught in a contradiction, because it also affirms that it wants nothing to do with the Church; and as in times past, it subjects the Church to all sorts of calumnies and persecutions.

Yet those same lips of Jesus which pronounced such golden words as "Consider the lilies of the field" (Mt. 6:28), "Love one another" (Jn. 15:17), and "Blessed are the pure in heart" (Mt. 5:8),

15

those very same lips one day affirmed: "You are Peter and on this rock I will build my Church" (Mt. 16:18) and "As the Father has sent me, even so I send you" (Jn. 20:21).

Whoever thinks of Christ without the Church is thinking of an imaginary person who never existed.

Yet perhaps this mistaken view, so widespread in the world today, does have a positive side. For those who admire Christ may one day reach the point of wanting to get to know him. And if, with confidence and love, they succeed in penetrating his heart, there they will find his spouse, the Church, which he founded, loved and nourished, and for which he gave his life.

But this is not yet the whole picture.

For if there is one thing that is worth more than anything else both in the Church as a whole, considered as the People of God, and in those who have the duty to pasture the flock in the place of Jesus, this something is the presence of Christ himself in the Church and in its ministers.

Hence, to fight against the Church is to fight against the very Person one claims to admire.

And since on the one hand, there are some who erroneously identify the Church with the hierarchy alone, and on the other hand, there are those who

16

mistakenly view the hierarchy as the cause of the Church's ills, I think we will find it worthwhile if we take the time to deepen our understanding of Christ's presence in the hierarchy.

Peter

This summer I visited the splendid little eleventh-century church of St. Peter in Clages, near Sion, Switzerland. There could have been no better place to meditate on the hierarchy.

In order to enter the church one must descend seven steps, and I thought of the foundation, the hidden rock, beneath.

"Jesus!" Suddenly I was deeply moved. "You were there in the tabernacle, and above you in a small, beautiful, stained glass window, Peter!"

What a mystery! I wished that he could speak, I would have liked to hear it all from him. I would have liked him to come to life and tell me how everything had happened. But I opened the New Testament to the Gospels, where the Holy Spirit has indelibly etched the extraordinary words Jesus addressed to Peter.

Jesus' Words to Peter

Peter's brother Andrew brings him to meet Jesus during the time when John is still baptizing. Catching sight of him, Jesus does not call Peter to follow him, but fixing his gaze on the fisherman he reveals God's plan for him. "'So you are Simon, the son of John? You shall be called Cephas ["Rock"]' (which translated is Peter)" (Jn. 1:42*).

The call will come another day. Jesus sees Simon and Andrew busy fishing and he says to them, "'Follow me and I will make you become fishers of men.' And immediately they left their nets and followed him" (Mk. 1:17-18).

But here, now, are the prophetic words which have all the solemnity of a foundation. Jesus had asked his apostles who the people thought he was. And Peter, filled with the Holy Spirit who acts best in those who love and believe, says: "You are the Christ, the Son of the living God" (Mt. 16:16). He has grasped the true reality of Jesus.

Moved by this answer, which could not have been revealed to Peter except by the Father, Jesus calls him "blessed." And with his heart overflowing with love for this man (who was predestined from the very beginning), he gives to the one who has given (Cf. Lk. 6:38; Mt. 13:12), and reveals to Peter who he is and what he is to do:

> You are Peter, and on this rock I will build my Church, and the powers of death shall not prevail against it. I will give you the keys of the kingdom of heaven, and whatever you bind on earth shall be bound in heaven, and whatever you loose on earth shall be loosed in heaven (Mt. 16:18-19).

"You are Peter."

In ancient texts of the Greek liturgy which have recently come to light, there are many expressions praising Peter:

> Peter, the unbreakable rock of the Church.

> The rock which is the foundation of the Church.

> Hail, foundation of the Church and unshakable ground, divine herald who has the keys of the kingdom of heaven.[1]

Leo the Great in the fifth century puts these words on the lips of Jesus:

"Blessed are you, Simon" (Mt. 16:17) . . . because . . . you did not let yourself be deceived by earthly thoughts . . . And as my Father has shown you my divinity, in the same way I will reveal to you your own greatness. "You are Peter": that is, even though I am the irremovable rock, the cornerstone which will make one sole people out of the Jews and pagans, . . . nonetheless you are also a rock because you have been given the same strength. So what I possess by virtue of the power [conferred on me], you have in common with me by participation . . . "And on this rock I will build my Church" (Mt. 16:18). On the firmness of this rock I will build an eternal temple.[2]

The Protestant theologian Cullman writes:

The rock, the foundation of all Churches of all time remains the historical Peter, the man whom Jesus had chosen, and singled out especially among the Twelve, as witness of his life, of his death, and as the first witness of his resurrection. It is on Peter that Christ, who is himself the cornerstone, will forever build his Church, as long as there is one on earth.[3]

And Paul VI considers the impression that this word "rock" might have on people in today's world. He says:

This meditation [about the rock] . . . arouses opposing sentiments in people. For some, a feeling of great joy, such as that of a shipwrecked sailor who reaches port, or a thinker who comes to the light, or the joy of a simple member of the faithful who knows he is on sure ground. But for others, the encounter with a truth authoritatively taught and sealed by unchangeable dogmas gives the disagreeable impression of an annoying and unjust imposition on thought. Why? Because it goes back to a secret of God: faith is an act of our spirit, which cannot be accomplished without a mysterious divine assistance, without a grace. Jesus notes this explicitly on the occasion of Peter's confession of the Messiah's divinity: "My father who is in heaven has revealed this to you" (Cf. Mt. 16:17).[4]

"And on this rock I will build my Church."

The words of Jesus are unequivocal. The rock on which he is building his Church is Peter. It is true that other passages in the New Testament refer to Jesus as the rock; and undoubtedly, he is the rock that the builders have rejected which has become the cornerstone of the Church. But Jesus will ascend to the right hand of the Father, and he needs to choose someone else who will function as a rock for his Church. And this is Peter. Moreover Jesus is not only the foundation stone of the Church; he is also the founder of the whole Church. And since he compares his Church to a building, here, with these words, he chooses the first stone.

"I will build." Jesus speaks of the future. While he is speaking to Peter he does not build his Church. He prepares it. The Church will be born visibly on Pentecost when the Holy Spirit will fill those men who have been destined to be the foundation of the Church.

Ambrose says, "Peter is the one to whom Jesus said 'You are Peter and on this rock I will build my Church' (Mt. 16:18). Therefore where Peter is, there is the Church. . . ."[5]

Meditating on the name "Peter," St. John Chrysostom is struck by the faith of Peter who recognizes Christ. "'On this rock I will build my Church', that is, on the faith shown in this confession. With these words [Jesus] indicates that

many one day will believe . . . and he constitutes
[the Apostle] shepherd of his Church. . . ."[6]

*"And the Powers of death shall not prevail
against it."*

The powers of death are synonymous with hell,
death. The Church will not die.

*"I will give you the keys of the kingdom of
heaven."*

The keys signify the power given to Peter to
procure access to the Kingdom of Heaven for
others. Having the keys, Peter represents the owner
of the house, to whom he is responsible. The keys
also signify the power to give the authentic
interpretation of the law of Jesus. It is Peter before
anyone else who will have to "teach them all that I
have commanded you" (Mt. 28:20).

*"Whatever you bind on earth shall be bound in
heaven, and whatever you loose on earth shall be
loosed in heaven."*

It is paradoxical! Heaven is subjecting itself to
the decisions of Peter on earth. But this is possible
only if in Peter it is Christ who lives. Heaven
cannot sanction anything other than what Christ

23

himself would have decided. And so we see expressed in these words, without any doubt, the luminous presence of Christ in Peter, head of the apostolic college, the first hierarchy of the Church.

If this is the way things are, then Catherine of Siena's expression: "Sweet Christ on earth,"[7] addressed to Peter's successors, is indeed true and theologically sound. The saints always know better!

Augustine put it this way: Peter baptizes, but it is Christ who baptizes . . .[8] And John Chrysostom asserted: "If someone thinks that this sacrifice [which Peter, Paul and others offer] is inferior to that [offered by Christ], he does not know that Christ is present and acting now as well." And Hilary of Poitiers concludes:

> The Lord has transmitted to the Apostles [and therefore — we say — first of all to Peter] all of his powers and all his efficacy. Those who in Adam were formed in the image and the likeness of God, now receive the perfect form and likeness with Christ, differing from their Lord in nothing, as far as effective power is concerned. And those who previously were earthly now become heavenly.[10]

Augustine has his own way of looking at Peter: in him who receives the keys he sees the whole Church. Therefore, for Augustine, Peter is synonymous with the Church. He says: "If when the Church excommunicates, the excommunication is ratified in heaven; and if the one who is reconciled with the Church is reconciled in heaven — if this happens in the Church, it means that Peter, when he received the keys, represented the Church."[11]

The power to bind and to loose given to Peter is also a power to teach. He declares a doctrine to be true or false, and proclaims a given practice to be licit or illicit.

It is also a power to govern. Peter can welcome persons into the community or put them out of it. The primitive Church quickly related this power with that of the forgiveness of sins through Baptism.

So far we have considered the promise of the primacy in Matthew's Gospel. But let us listen to some other words spoken by Jesus to Peter as recorded by Luke: "Simon, Simon, behold, Satan demanded to have you all, that he might sift you like wheat, but I have prayed for you that your faith may not fail; and when you have turned again, strengthen your brothers" (Lk. 22:31-32*).

Jesus is about to die, and he knows that when the shepherd has been struck the sheep will be scattered. So he turns to Peter and asks for his cooperation, addressing him with the most astonishing words: "But I have prayed for you that your faith may not fail."

"I have prayed for you."

Generally it is men who pray to Jesus. But the stakes here are too high: the Church is a divine work. Jesus feels the need to sustain it, and he sustains it sustaining Peter, praying for him as if the salvation of all depended on the faithfulness of Peter.

"And when you have turned again, strengthen your brothers."

Jesus entrusts the Apostles to Peter. Peter is the center of unity, the head; and what he says will be true. The first Vatican Council cited this text in affirming the infallibility of the pope.

Peter is an instrument of God, and therefore God himself will act in him. But precisely because of this, we can apply to him Paul's words: "God chose what is foolish in the world . . . God chose what is weak in the world . . . so that no human being might boast in the presence of God" (1 Cor. 1:27-29).

Indeed, we notice in Peter the weakness and instability characteristic of human nature. Side by side with his great faith, is the fear at times of adhering to that faith, or the sin of not giving witness to it. We see his generous heart filled with love; yet he even reaches the point of denying the person whom he loves. He is impulsive and slow to comprehend the true spirit of his Master, which is not one of command, but of service. When Jesus reveals his passion, for instance, Peter does not want to accept God's plan. Jesus is forced to say to him: "Get behind me, Satan! You are an obstacle in my path, because the way you think is not God's way but man's" (Mt. 16:23*). And when, called by Jesus, he walks upon the waters, he becomes frightened and sinks: faith, and the fear of adhering to it.

Peter is sincerely generous; but as yet he is too human and therefore vulnerable: "And [Peter] said to him, 'Lord I am ready to go with you to prison and to death.' Jesus said, 'I tell you, Peter, the cock will not crow this day, until you three times deny that you know me'" (Lk. 22:33-34).

In contrast to this weakness, this temperament made of highs and lows (rather like that of all of us poor mortals), what emerges majestically is the moving, adamant faithfulness of Jesus to the man he has chosen. We find it described for us in John's gospel:

> When they had finished breakfast, Jesus said to Simon Peter, "Simon, son of John, do you love me more than these?" He said to him, "Yes, Lord; you know that I love you." [Jesus] said to him, "Feed my lambs." A second time he said to him, "Simon, son of John, do you love me?" [Peter] said to him, "Yes, Lord; you know that I love you." [Jesus] said to him, "Tend my sheep." He said to him the third time, "Simon, son of John, do you love me?" Peter was grieved because he said to him the third time, "Do you love me?" And he said to him, "Lord, you know everything; you know that I love you." Jesus said to him, "Feed my sheep" (Jn. 21:15-17).

"Simon, do you love me more than these?"

Peter has again found communion with Jesus. This is beautiful. This is consoling. It tells us that even if we make mistakes, once we have changed our ways, Jesus no longer remembers the past, but sees us in the light of God's plan for us. How wonderful God's mercy is! This is Christianity! As Peter Chrysologus writes:

Being obliged to return to heaven, [Christ] entrusted his sheep to Peter, to pasture them in his place. And in order not to force with authority this weak beginning of his conversion, but rather to help him with kindness, he repeated to Peter, 'Do you love me? Feed my sheep.'[12]

Commenting on these words of Jesus, Paul VI says:

That "more" ("Do you love me *more*") demands . . . and arouses a primacy of love. . . . Together with this primacy of authority already conferred on Simon Peter, Jesus desires a corresponding primacy of love. . . . [He must be] first in loving Christ in order to be first in governing the Church; that is, first in loving the Church.[13]

"Lord, you know everything; you know that I love you."

Tempered by the humiliation of the test he so sadly failed, Peter abandons himself totally to Jesus. If Jesus confirms it, then he feels he can say that he loves him. It is a threefold question of love which seems designed to evoke a threefold declaration of love in order to cancel out the threefold denial.

It is an enchanting, solemn scene. Jesus transmits his own mission to Peter. "I am the good shepherd" (Jn. 10:11), he had said. After Jesus' death Peter will have to take his place. Jesus' flock is entrusted to him. And Peter will never forget that in order to feed the flock he was asked to love.

Peter at Pentecost

On the day of Pentecost the Holy Spirit descends and the apostles are completely transformed, Peter as well. Weakness gives way to unyielding strength; ignorance to the rapture of wisdom. His heart is on fire. He is no longer himself; it is Christ who lives in him. He gives his first marvelous discourse and, among other things, says:

"Men of Israel hear these words. Jesus of Nazareth, a man attested to you by God with mighty works and wonders and signs . . . you crucified and killed by the hands of lawless men. . . . This Jesus God raised up, and of that we all are witnesses. Being therefore exalted at the right hand of God, and having received from the Father the promise of the Holy Spirit, he has poured out this which you see and hear. . . ."

Now when they heard this they were cut to the heart, and said to Peter and the rest of the apostles: "Brothers, what shall we do?" And Peter . . . testified with many other words and exhorted them, saying, "Save yourselves from this crooked generation." So those who received his word were baptized, and there were added that day about three thousand souls (Acts 2:22-23, 32-33, 37, 40-41).

Peter and the First Christian Community

In this way the first Christian community was born. In the Acts we find that "all who believed were together and had all things in common . . . having favor with all the people" (Acts 2:44, 47).

Peter works miracles, and among these is the healing of the lame man, to whom he says, "I have no silver and gold but I give you what I have. In the name of Jesus Christ of Nazareth, walk" (Acts 3:6).

And the Acts go on to say: "More than ever believers were added to the Lord, multitudes both of men and women, so that they even carried out the sick into the streets, and laid them on beds and pallets, that as Peter came by at least his shadow might fall on some of them" (Acts 5:14-15).

Peter's Role as Leader

From the very beginning Peter's role is one of leadership: he is the head of the community in Jerusalem. And as the representative of Christ and of the Church he applies the powers he has received, by punishing the deceit of Ananias and Sapphira, and bestowing the gift of the Holy Spirit on the new converts in Samaria.

Moreover, Peter is also considered the head of the Church in the eyes of the world. It is he who defends the Gospel before the Jewish authorities, and he is the one imprisoned as the person principally responsible for the young Church.

And with the conversion of Cornelius, the Roman centurion, it is Peter who opens up the spreading of the Gospel to "all nations" (Cf. Mt. 28:19).

Peter's preeminence, his function as the rock, and his office as the one who guarantees the unity of the Church, are universally recognized in the Church of the New Testament. His name appears first in all the lists of the apostles.

Peter is one of the Twelve, but he is also the first apostle to witness the risen Christ. Paul attests to this only a few years after the resurrection: "He appeared first to Cephas and secondly to the twelve" (1 Cor. 15:5). And that definitely confirms Peter's place at the head of the people of God: Peter is the head of the Twelve. Furthermore, the apostle that Paul wants to see is Peter.

The incident at Antioch shows Peter in a moment of weakness, and Paul rebukes him. Christ lives in Peter, but this life has a progression; and it reaches an ever greater continuity as his mission advances.

Peter's Martyrdom

Before Jesus washed the feet of the apostles,

Peter had perhaps been dreaming of a triumphant Messiah. Instead Jesus presented him with the countenance of the suffering Servant (Cf. Is. 52:13). The life Peter is to lead, therefore, must be like that of Jesus: a life of love, service and choosing the cross. For it is in love that the primacy of Peter will have to be exercised.

And he will be faithful. His love will be similar to that of Jesus; he will give his life for his sheep. Jesus had told him:

"Truly, truly, I say to you, when you were young, you girded yourself and walked where you would; but when you are old, you will stretch out your hands, and another will gird you and carry you where you do not wish to go." (This he said to show by what death he was to glorify God.) and after this he said to him, "Follow me" (Jn. 21:18-19).

"Follow me": it is the invitation to the martyrdom he will undergo in Rome. As Gregory of Nyssa says:

Through a martyrdom which culminated in a way not unlike the passion of the Lord, the one whom the Lord had designated as prince and leader of the apostolic choir acquired a glory befitting his dignity. . . . He . . . is the firm and most solid rock upon which the Savior has built the Church.[14]

2.

The Twelve

"Lord, before going on, I want to speak to you.

"You see, Jesus, I feel that your choice of the Twelve concerns me as well, even though it took place on a particular day long ago; not only because I am a daughter of the Church, but because — with your grace — I have and want nothing but you.

"So everything that concerns you, even if it seems distant to others, is present for me. For you, who love me now; you, who after two thousand years have now become — through your immense goodness — the purpose of my life — you are the same Jesus you were then. You have never spiritually left the Church you founded. You live within it, and your presence renders it eternally young, ever present, always new.

"Explain to me then, Jesus, what you intended to do that day; and tell me something about these twelve men you singled out from the rest of the world.

"I will be listening to you as I read about you and them in the New Testament."

The Choosing of the Twelve

The selecting of the apostles is one of the most significant acts of Jesus' public life.

In those days he went out into the hills to pray; and all night he continued in prayer to God. And when it was day, he called his disciples, and chose from them twelve, whom he named apostles: Simon, whom he named Peter, and Andrew his brother, and James and John, and Philip, and Bartholomew, and Matthew, and Thomas, and James the son of Alphaeus, and Simon who was called the Zealot, and Judas the son of James, and Judas Iscariot, who became a traitor (Lk. 6:12-16).

These twelve are called to have a personal relationship with Jesus. He wants them to be his companions. They share the life he leads; and with him they constitute a community, which is much more like that of a founder with his first companions than that of a teacher with his disciples.

They are with him throughout his earthly career, so that they may be direct witnesses of his words and actions, and, later on, of his resurrection.[1]

The Foundation of the Church

The apostles are considered the foundation of the Church. In the book of Revelation we find: "The wall of the city had twelve foundations, and on them the twelve names of the twelve apostles of the Lamb" (Rev. 21:14). And Gregory the Great writes that the apostles are the "foundation set in the ground as the first solid base."[2]

Augustine, pondering: "In what sense are the apostles and the prophets a foundation?", replies: "In that their authority sustains our weakness."[3]

The Twelve as a "Communion," and Paul

The apostles were chosen by Jesus who said, "Did I not choose you, the Twelve?" (Jn. 6:70). And again: "You did not choose me, but I chose you" (Jn. 15:16).

He chose them individually, but they must consider themselves a "body"; and as such they have been invested with their functions.

Mark wrote, "And so he appointed the Twelve" (Mk. 3:16*). This number is meant to symbolize universality. And as the patriarchs were the fathers of the twelve tribes of the chosen people of the Old Testament, so the twelve apostles are the founders of the new people of God.

The apostles are aware of being a very special group. This is shown by the fact that Peter considers it indispensable to maintain the number of twelve; and after Jesus' ascension, he proposes choosing a substitute for Judas (Cf. Acts 1:21-26).

The Second Vatican Council formally declared that the Lord constituted them "after the manner of a college or a fixed group,"[4] clarifying however, that this is not to be understood in terms of a group of equals who delegate one of their number to the presidency, since the origin of Peter's role is quite different. In the institution of the apostolic college, therefore, we find the mark of unity and the reality of a communion.

And in order that this unity might always be alive and perfect, it is to the apostles themselves that Jesus gives the new commandment at the Last Supper: "This is my commandment, that you love one another as I have loved you" (Jn. 15:12).

Only by putting this commandment into practice, will the apostles be able to keep alive their vocation to be one body and experience all the supernatural effects of the presence of Christ, who is there wherever this commandment is lived.

The Twelve can act only in strict communion.[5] At the Council of Jerusalem the apostles express themselves in these words: "It has seemed good to the Holy Spirit and to us . . ." (Acts 15:28). The decisions are made in unity.

Jesus desires that everything involving the hierarchy of the new Church be done in unity. And it is in unity that he can reign, for Jesus is the true head of the Church: "But you are not to be called 'rabbi', for you have one teacher, and you are all brothers. . . . Neither be called 'masters' ['leaders'], for you have one master, the Christ" (Mt. 23:8, 10*).

Paul calls himself equal to the Twelve as regards mission and authority. They were apostles before him, but not more so (Cf. Galatians 1:1,17).

The Doctrinal Authority of the Twelve

The Twelve were always clearly distinct from the rest of the disciples; and what emerged above all was their doctrinal authority. It is written in fact that ". . . [the baptized] devoted themselves to the apostles' teaching . . ." (Acts 2:42).[6]

The Twelve are first sent to the children of Israel: to preach that the kingdom of God is near; to heal the sick and the lepers; to cast out demons; and to raise the dead. If their word is listened to, it brings peace; if it is not, they must shake the dust from their sandals. Speaking of the Twelve, Gregory the Great has this to say:

And — since the holy doctors . . . in their preaching are open to those who receive the word, but with their authority are closed to those who resist — the apostles are rightly called doors. . . . The door of the Church is Peter, who received [Cornelius] who was searching for the faith, and who cast out Simon [the magician] who wanted to buy the power of miracles. To Cornelius he said: "Truly I perceive that God shows no partiality" (Acts 10:34). And he benevolently opened up to him the secrets of the kingdom. To the latter [Simon the magician], with the words "your silver perish with you" (Acts 8:20). . . he closed the entrance to the heavenly dwelling.[7]

44

The Twelve Act as Jesus Did

The Twelve act in a certain way as Jesus did.[8] He preached; so must they. He is the shepherd, and so are Peter and the others. Christ had to suffer, and his disciples likewise will be persecuted. Christ died for his own, and his disciples must be ready for the same destiny. They are called to be another Christ.

How to View the Hierarchy

The world criticizes and judges the hierarchy — of which the apostles are the first expression — as a rigid organ of government with authoritarian powers, which dominates the faithful, demanding that they renounce reason in order to believe only what the hierarchy thinks, and do what it establishes.

This is the worst possible caricature of that marvelous reality which is God's design for the hierarchy.

It is true that in the course of history, various men — invested by Christ as his ministers — have not carried out their mission worthily. They have betrayed the Gospel, paying more heed to the honor bestowed on them than to their duties and responsibilities, and viewing their mission more as one of power than one of service.

But if we stop to think that we are all sinners, and that we must first of all judge ourselves, we will be much more serene in considering that the apostles — and after them the bishops — have had one vocation alone in which they were to mirror themselves: Christ's. And certainly the great majority of the ministers whom God has chosen throughout these twenty centuries have strived to imitate this model.

If a certain number have strayed from following Christ's example, we must remember that even while Jesus was still on earth, he was not able to avert the betrayal of Judas, because of the freedom with which every human being is endowed.

We must do everything in our power to eradicate from the world this deformed idea of the hierarchy of the Church, so that it might be seen as it is: vested with the highest dignity; possessed of powers we could call divine; and created to serve others and to save them — another Christ.

The Presence of Christ in the Apostles

To the apostles Jesus had said, "He who hears you hears me, and he who rejects you rejects me" (Lk. 10:16), and that is enough to attest that Jesus is in the apostles.

"He who receives you receives me" (Mt. 10:40): whoever receives the apostles receives Christ. In the early Church everyone was convinced of this.

Jesus gives certain powers to the apostles with the words: "In truth I say to you, whatever you bind on earth shall be bound in heaven and whatever you loose on earth shall be loosed also in heaven" (Mt. 18:18). In the Church's decisions therefore, God's decisions are being carried out.[9] Just as in the case of Peter, if it were not Christ acting in the apostles, in binding and in loosing, heaven could not possibly sanction what is done. This is another demonstration that Christ is present in the apostles. As André Lemaire says:

The ministers of Christ, therefore, are his representatives, invested with powers by him; to receive them means to receive Christ.[10]

If we understand the reality of the minister's

authority, there is sufficient reason to be struck with fear and admiration before "such power given to men" (Mt. 9:8). Actually, the temptation is great to make them semi-gods (Cf. Acts 10:25-26; 14:11-15). But nothing would be more contrary to the Gospel. [11]

The Powers of the Apostles

After the resurrection Jesus confirms the mission he has already given the apostles, but he broadens its scope to include the whole world. Matthew concludes his Gospel with these words of Jesus:

"All authority in heaven and on earth has been given to me. Go, therefore, and make desciples of all nations, baptizing them in the name of the Father and of the Son and of the Holy Spirit, teaching them to observe all that I have commanded you; and know that I am with you always, until the end of time" (Mt. 28:18-20*).

Mark speaks of further signs which will accompany their preaching: "They will cast out demons; they will speak in new tongues; they will pick up serpents, and if they drink any deadly thing, it will not hurt them . . ." (Mk. 16:17-18).

But let us continue with Matthew's account: "All authority in heaven and on earth has been given to me." Because of this Jesus can give powers to those he has chosen.

The apostles will have to "make disciples"; and here we can anticipate the power of governing. They will have to "baptize"; and here we see the power to sanctify. And they will have to "teach" everything that they have learned; and here is the power of prophecy.

The apostles knew the truth; Jesus had revealed it to them. As Tertullian says:

"Could any truth remain hidden to a Peter, who was called the rock on which the Church would be built, and who was provided with the keys of the Kingdom of Heaven, with the power to loose and to bind in heaven and on earth?

"Could any truth remain hidden to a John, who was so dear to the Lord as to rest on his breast, and who was the only one to whom the Lord revealed the betrayal of Judas, and who was then given to Mary as her son in place of Jesus?

"What could he have hidden from persons to whom he showed his glory, with the vision of Moses and Elijah, and whom he allowed to hear the voice of the Father coming down from heaven?" [12]

And elsewhere he writes:

"If the Lord Jesus Christ sent the apostles to preach, it is evident that one must not receive other preachers. . . . And this because no one else knows the Father but the Son and those to whom the Son has revealed him. But we know that the Son . . . has revealed him to the apostles. . . ."

. . . Only that doctrine should be considered true which is in agreement with the doctrine of the apostolic churches, the mothers and wellsprings of the faith. [13]

In the words of Maximus of Turin:

Christ our Lord can be known only through

the mouths of the apostles and the doctrine of the disciples; . . . after the bitterness of the law, the apostles — like chalices of the Sacrament — distill sweetness from their veins with abundant wisdom. The apostles are fountains which have irrigated the face of the earth with their doctrine.[14]

"And know that I am with you always until the end of time." Perhaps Jesus has never spoken so explicitly about his presence with and in the apostles. The theologian Bouyer states:

It is the historic Christ . . . who acts through the 'ministries' that he has given personally to his Church, beginning with that of the apostles. . . . Because of the living bond which they have with him [their communion with him], these ministries guarantee that it will always be he, through his Spirit, who in every age will nourish, maintain and develop the Church itself as his Body. [15]

The Apostles' Mission to Continue Jesus

Jesus addresses the apostles with words that reveal the lofty dignity of their calling: "As the Father has sent me, even so I send you" (Jn. 20:21).

"As": this is one of the famous "as's" which make the Gospel so attractive because they bring the reality of heaven to earth. For example: "Love your neighbor *as* yourself" (Mt. 19:18). This is a law from heaven; it is the way the persons of the Trinity love—a way which man is not accustomed to by nature, but to which he must adapt through grace.

"You, therefore, must be perfect, *as* your heavenly Father is perfect" (Mt. 5:48). In those moments in which Jesus lives in a Christian, the Christian is perfect as the Father is perfect.

Now, Jesus has just said to the apostles: "*As* the Father has sent me, even so I send you." But in sending Jesus, the Father had a precise plan in mind; a definite goal to reach. So then, an identical goal is destined for the apostles.

". . .I send you": The apostles receive their mandate from Christ.

"And when he had said this, he breathed on them, and said to them, 'Receive the Holy Spirit' " (Jn. 20:22).

Breathing upon the apostles, Jesus transmits his life to them. They are re-created in view of their function of continuing the Father's design, which he expressed in sending the Son: the reconciliation of humanity with God.

"If you forgive the sins of any, they are forgiven; if you retain the sins of any, they are retained" (Jn. 20:23).

The apostles will be able to forgive sins, something which up to now has been the direct prerogative of God. This is the institution of the Sacrament of Reconciliation.

Jesus, therefore, wants us to have our sins forgiven through other human beings: his ministers. These ministers represent him, and in them it is he who absolves: Jesus present in the apostles. Later Paul will say, "So we are ambassadors for Christ, God making his appeal through us" (2 Cor. 5:20).

The Apostles' Mission to Serve

As with Jesus, every act of the apostles will be an act of service. "Whoever would be great among you must be your servant. . . . even as the Son of Man came not to be served but to serve, and to give his life as a ransom for many" (Mt. 20:26, 28).

Ambrose says "The apostles were commanded not to carry a staff. . .an external sign of authority and a painful instrument of punishment . . . . [The Master] had sent them to sow the faith, not by force but through teaching; not by show of authority, but emphasizing the doctrine of humility."[16]

The Holy Spirit and the Apostles

At Pentecost the Holy Spirit communicated power to the apostles when, under the form of tongues of fire (Cf. Acts 2:1-4), he lit the flame of divine love in their hearts. And as we see in Acts, once having received the gift of the Spirit, they had the ability to grant it to others.

Now when the apostles at Jerusalem heard that Samaria had received the word of God, they sent to them Peter and John, who came down and prayed for them that they might receive the Holy Spirit; for it had not yet fallen on any of them, but they had only been baptized in the name of the Lord Jesus.

Then they laid their hands on them and they received the Holy Spirit (Acts 8:14-17).

And through their preaching, they communicated the life that they were living: "That which we have seen and heard we proclaim also to you, so that you may have fellowship with us . . ." (1 Jn. 1:3).

Moreover the apostles acted as the ministers of the sacrament of the Eucharist, having been designated for this office by Jesus when he said, "Do this in remembrance of me" (Lk. 22:19).

Jesus' Prayer for the Apostles

Jesus is about to go to his death and then to rise again. God's plan for him is coming to fulfillment, and with it, God's plan for the small group of apostles.

The tragedy of his death could scatter this

handful of men, whom he has succeeded in drawing away from the world in order to make them "Kingdom of Heaven", "Church", "Mystical Body". But instead his very death will be the cause of their birth.

It is to the apostles that Jesus especially dedicates his last prayer to the Father, even though he then extends it to all those who through them will believe.

"As you Father, are in me, and I in you, may they also be one in us" (Jn. 17:21*).

Jesus prays to the Father (and it is God praying to God; and therefore he obtains what he asks for) that as the Father is in him and he is in the Father, so also may the apostles be one in them. But if the apostles are in the unity of the Father and the Son, then the Trinity-God − is in the apostles.

"The glory which you have given me I have given to them, that they may be one even as we are one" (Jn. 17:22*).

Jesus has transmitted all that he is to his apostles, revealing to them that he is the Word, and making them sharers in the divine life which the Father has given to him. And with this, they can be one: one with him, with the Father, and among themselves.

"I in them and you in me, that they may become perfectly one, so that the world may know that you have sent me and have loved them even as you have loved me" (Jn. 17:23*).

"I in them": Jesus asks to be present in the apostles.

"And you in me": and the Father in Jesus. But the unity of the Father with Jesus is perfect; so if the apostles are in that unity, they will experience its perfection.

"So that the world may know that you have sent me": the world will know that the Father has sent Jesus because it will see him alive in the apostles.

"And have loved them even *as* you have loved me": it is another "as" from the Gospel which brings the standards of heaven's way of life to earth. And this is as it should be. For with Jesus, the Kingdom of Heaven has come to earth.

"I have made known to them your name, and I will make it known, that the love with which you have loved me may be in them, and I in them" (Jn. 17:26).

"And I will make it known": Jesus will continue to reveal the Father to the apostles through his presence in them, and through the Holy Spirit which he will send.

"That the love with which you have loved me may be in them": Jesus loves his neighbor as himself, and asks the Father to love the apostles as he has loved him. It is enough to make one's head spin; it is purely divine!

"And I in them": Jesus concludes his stupendous prayer asking nothing less than his presence in the apostles.

3.

God's Ambassadors

Who are the Bishops?

The bishops are the successors of the apostles; and are bound through the apostolic succession to Jesus Christ himself, who creates them when they are consecrated, and who lives and acts in them. For the bishops are instuments of salvation; and salvation cannot come but from Christ. As the Second Vatican Council states:

In the bishops . . . our Lord Jesus Christ . . . is present in the midst of those who believe. For sitting at the right hand of God the Father, He is not absent from the gathering of His high priests [bishops],[2] . . . He is preaching the Word . . . and constantly administering the sacraments of faith to those who believe. By their paternal role (Cf. 1 Cor. 4:15), He incorporates new members . . . and finally . . . He directs and guides the people. . . .

For the discharging of such great duties, the apostles were enriched by Christ with a special outpouring of the Holy Spirit . . . (Cf. Acts 1:8;

2:4; Jn. 20:22-23). This spiritual gift they passed on to their helpers by the imposition of hands (Cf. 1 Tim. 4:14; 2 Tim. 1:6-7), and it has been transmitted down to us in episcopal consecration. . . . by episcopal consecration is conferred the fullness of the sacrament of orders. . . .

. . . For from tradition . . . both of the East and of the West, it is clear that, by means of the imposition of hands and the words of consecration, the grace of the Holy Spirit is so conferred, and the sacred character so impressed, that bishops in an eminent and visible way undertake Christ's own role as Teacher, Shepherd, and High Priest. . . .[3]

The bishop's authority, therefore, comes from above, from Christ. And consequently it is inconceivable that a bishop be created from below, by the people, democratically — even though, at times, the faithful may assist in the choosing of the person. The bishop cannot be created from below for a very simple reason: any group is always limited, and a person delegated by a particular group — even an extremely large group — cannot be a bishop. For as the theologian Bouyer writes:

The local church, in an invisible but real

manner, calls forth and gathers to itself the universal Church of all time, the one total body of Christ. Consequently, a so-called democratic ministry will never be truly representative . . . of the whole Church, if in fact it represents only those who are visibly gathered in a given place.[4]

In a democratic conception of the Church, the bishop would come to represent only the present members of his own church, whereas he is called to represent the Church in its entirety throughout history — that is, the whole Communion of Saints, including all those who have ever lived and all those yet to be born, together with its Head, the risen Christ. "It follows," continues Bouyer, "that it would not be possible to have an ecclesiastical ministry capable of representing the whole body of the Church, if first of all it did not represent its Head, if it did not emanate from the Head itself . . ."[5]

As the whole of scripture teaches us, such a ministry can only come from heaven.

Living the reality of the Church, one may have experienced through a special grace, that there, in a particular place where the Church is present, there are all the saints who have ever lived: all those of the

New Testament, on back to Ann and Joachim and the saints of the Old Testament, and back through the centuries to the prophets and patriarchs, all the way to Adam; as well as all those who will ever be.

These experiences, which should be considered secondary in comparison to the teachings of our faith, are, however, a useful stimulant to live more intensely the wonderful, mysterious, and consoling life of the Church. This life associates us — particularly during the Eucharistic liturgy — with all our fellow Christians throughout the world, with those of the future and those of the past, including all those who were dear to us.

The Apostolic Succession

At the beginning of this chapter, I mentioned apostolic succession. Let us now see from authoritative witnesses how this succession has always been decisive throughout the history of the Church in determining the authenticity of bishops. Clement of Rome, pope from 92 to 101, in his first letter to the Corinthians says:

The apostles received the gospel for us from

the Lord Jesus Christ; Jesus, the Christ, was sent from God. Thus Christ is from God and the apostles from Christ. In both instances the orderly procedure depends on God's will.[6]

Here is where the apostolic succession is rooted: in God. Christ is from God, and the apostles from Christ. And Clement continues:

And so the apostles, after receiving their orders and being fully convinced by the resurrection of our Lord Jesus Christ and assured by God's word, went out in the confidence of the Holy Spirit to preach the good news that God's Kingdom was about to come. They preached in country and city, and appointed their first converts, after testing them by the Spirit, to be the bishops and deacons of future believers.[7]

So Christ is from God, the apostles from Christ, and the bishops from the apostles.

In the second century Irenaeus affirms. "[The presbyters — synonymous in this case with bishops] have the apostolic succession and, with succession in the episcopate, they have received the sure charism of the truth. . . ."[8]

Before the ascension, Jesus had said, "Know that I am with you always, until the end of time" (Mt. 28:20*). So that he could "remain", the apostles had to have successors, and these successors were those on whom they laid their hands. Tertullian, also living in the second century, wrote:

It may be that there are heresies which dare to claim that they date back to the apostolic times. . . . Let them produce documents of the birth of their churches . . . the lists of their bishops . . . [that show] their succession from the very beginning, so as to show that the one who was the first bishop received his investiture from, and was preceded by, one of the apostles, or at least a man close to the apostles who had had constant contact with them. This is the way in which the apostolic churches show their qualifications: in this way the Church of Smyrna shows that Polycarp was appointed to that diocese by John; and in this way the Church of Rome shows that Clement was ordained by Peter. . . .[9]

The Catholic Church has had the immense fortune to have always been in the line of this succession.

Paul VI, in his discourse at Bombay in 1964, after the consecration of the new bishops, said,

> Let us take note of the event that is now taking place by means of our hands, transformed into instruments of the hands of God: that is, the event of the transmission. We have transmitted the fullness of the Priesthood of Jesus Christ to these our Brothers, who from now on we will call Bishops.
>
> We have transfused into them the Holy Spirit. We have transmitted to them our episcopal powers. We have associated them with us in our mission . . . to evangelize . . . to sanctify . . . and to guide. [10]

Everything comes to life and develops from a seed — even in the Church. And the seed of the hierarchy was sown by Jesus in the hearts of Peter and the apostles. But just as every seed needs time in order to develop, so every design of God needs time before it can fully express its richness and act with all its power.

This we ourselves see from the Work of God in which we work as instruments. Everything was contained in the seed, but it took decades to gradually understand what kind of tree would develop from it. And we are still on the path of discovery.

Similarly it took time for the early Church to come to a full understanding of what was supposed to be the function of Peter and his successors, and of the apostles and their successors.

The Church in the Apostolic Communities

As we can see in the New Testament, the apostles transmitted the heart of their role to the bishops. They wanted to assure the presence of Christ at the head of the Christian community.

Naturally, the apostles alone possess the prerogative of being the foundation of the Church. For the bishops exist in a Church which is already founded, so their function is to care for it and extend it.

In the first century, we see the apostles establishing the Church. In the second century, we find the bishops occupying the places vacated by the apostles. But between these two periods there is a time of transition.

The *Didache* or *The Lord's Teaching to the*

Gentiles transmitted by the Twelve Apostles, which is believed to date from the first century, reflects this period in which the hierarchy of the individual churches is unfolding in an apparently confused manner (as when the root comes forth from a seed, and then the various leaves emerge, first fused as one, and then separating). For instance, in certain areas there were two or more bishops in the same place.

The Twelve, scattered throughout the world to announce the joyful news, were helped by various charismatic persons, who are presented to us by the *Didache* in this way: "Let every apostle [a term used not only to indicate the Twelve] who comes to you be received as the Lord."[11] We find, therefore, that there were apostles, who assisted the Twelve in their preaching; and there was a living faith in Jesus' words: "He who receives you receives me" (Mt. 10:40).

"You shall not tempt any prophet who speaks in the Spirit, or judge him .... "[12] So there were also prophets; that is, faithful who were enriched with extraordinary gifts for the edification of the Christian community.

"Likewise, a true teacher is worthy, as a workman, of his food" (Cf. Mt. 10:10).[13] And there were also teachers, catechists who would travel around, stopping for a time in various places to give instructions in the truths of the faith.

In those communities already established, besides these apostles, prophets and teachers, we find established bishops and deacons, who pass judgment on the orthodoxy and the morality of those possessing these other charisms. "Elect therefore for yourselves bishops and deacons worthy of the Lord . . . they are the honored men among you along with the prophets and teachers." [14]

In the first decades of the Church, it seems that the terms *presbyteros* (Greek: "presbyter", "elder") and *episkopos* (Greek: "guardian", "overseer") were used almost synonymously. Or more precisely, in the Christian communities in Asia Minor, begun under the influence of John the Apostle, every group of so-called presbyters was sustained by an *episkopos*. The *episkopos* was the center of union of the community, and had the power of the "laying of hands"; that is, of conferring Holy Orders. In these communities, therefore, the presbyters were simply priests.

In the European communities, by contrast, which were under the influence of Paul, the so-called presbyters also had the office of bishop, whereas the center of union and the one who conferred Holy Orders was Paul or one of his more intimate co-workers (Titus, Timothy, etc.).

But this type of structure quickly developed into that already existing in the East. And so we find the system of bishops, priests and deacons already established during the second century.

At that time, the Christian population was mostly concentrated in the cities. In every city there was a bishop, who was the true head of the local church, the center of union, minister of the liturgy and the sacraments, and the only one in charge of preaching. The presbyters formed his council; and the deacons helped him materially during the sacred liturgy and in the performance of charitable works.

Ignatius, the greatest of the Apostolic Fathers, bishop of Antioch from the year 70 to 107, can be called the first doctor of the episcopate because he outlines its essential points. "According to Ignatius of Antioch, the hierarchy is less a juridical body, and more a charism for the Church, by means of which the members [of the Church] must reach sanctification." [15]

Regarding the episcopate, he affirms that the "bishop of all," [16] that is, the invisible Head of the whole Church throughout the world, is God or Jesus Christ. This is echoed in *the Episcopal Ministry,* the recent document of the ecumenical Group of Dombes, which is of significant ecumenical value:

God's design as attested to in the biblical revelation [of the Old Testament] underlines the *episcope* [that is, the role of pastoral vigilance and guardian of unity] of the Lord over his people. The Lord frees his people and gathers them together in view of his universal mission. He visits them, nourishes them and guides them.[17]

In the Old Testament, therefore, the Bishop of all is the Lord. "In the new covenant," continues the Document, "Jesus Christ, sent by the Father, fulfills this role of *episcope.*"[18] Hence, the Bishop is Jesus Christ.

According to Ignatius, the earthly bishop "has the role of the Father"[19] and "acts in the place of God."[20] He also refers to him as the "bishop who is seen,"[21] or "your bishop in this world,"[22] since the invisible, spiritual Bishop is Jesus.

For Ignatius, therefore, the episcopate is a divine

function attributed to the Father and to the Son, in which the bishops of the "catholic" (an adjective used for the first time by Ignatius) Church are made sharers. The idea of Jesus as bishop is derived from the first letter of Peter: "For you were straying like sheep, but have now returned to the Shepherd [Christ] and Guardian [*episcopos*] of your souls" (1 Pt. 2:25). In Ignatius, the word *episcopos* has already acquired a definite technical meaning as "bishop."

How a Bishop Should Be

The Fathers of the Church — almost all of them bishops — have left us precious words which illustrate how a bishop should be. Let us listen to Jerome:

"Be subject to one another out of reverence for Christ" (Eph. 5:21). Let the bishops listen to these words . . . to be subject to their subjects. . . . The Savior also assumed the condition of a slave (Cf. Phil. 2:7) in order to serve his disciples. . . . This is the difference between the pagan princes and the Christian ones; the former dominate their subjects; we instead are servants of our subjects. . . .[23]

Let [the bishop] be impartial toward all in giving commands; and, imitating the Apostle, let him put himself at everyone's disposal. . . . The one who receives them is not receiving them . . . but is above all receiving the One whose bishops they are. But when they are so honored, they should not claim anything more! We know that they must be fathers, and not masters. . . .[24]

We particularly like the following affirmation of Peter Chrysologus because it emphasizes that the teaching of the Gospel must be accompanied by Gospel living (Cf. Acts 1:1).

The teaching magisterium presupposes knowledge, but the authority of the magisterium is based on life. The one who does what he teaches makes the listener obedient. The true norm of doctrine is to teach with deeds. The doctrine administered with words is knowledge; that communicated through deeds is virtue. True knowledge, therefore, is knowledge united to virtue. That knowledge is divine, not human. [25]

Gregory the Great admonishes the bishops to "be careful that you do not become proud . . ." [26] And he writes:

> We exhort [you] to show yourselves so gentle toward the faithful that they may be more inclined to love your uprightness than to fear it. . . . Endeavor to correct their abuses in such a way that the paternal affection in your soul may never weaken. Be . . . busy with zeal for order, so that the wolf with its snares may not succeed in throwing the Lord's flock into confusion. . . . [27]
>
> In the life of the shepherds there is another thing . . . that grieves me much: . . . we have allowed ourselves to be carried away by earthly affairs; and, while we accept the [episcopal] ministry because of ambition, in reality we exercise another. . . . Those who were entrusted to us draw away from us, and we are silent. . . . Dearest brothers, I think that God cannot receive from others a greater insult than he receives from the bishops, when he sees that . . . we sin, we who were supposed to destroy sins. [28]

But of all the saints, it seems to me that Catherine of Siena ranks first in her ardent desire to see the bishops and cardinals worthy of their vocation. Her times were very sad times for the Church, and her words reflect it. To Cardinal Jacomo degli Orsini she writes:

You [bishops] have been chosen and drawn from the world and placed in the holy Church as mirrors in which the laity should find a model for themselves. You are flowers and columns in the garden of the holy Church.

But you must be fragrant flowers, not foul-smelling ones, clothed in the whiteness of purity, with the fragrance of patience and the most ardent charity, which comes from a heart, not narrow but large and generous, having learned from the first Truth, Who out of the greatness of His heart, gave His life. This is the fragrance with which you must perfume the sweet spouse of Christ . . .

I said that you are a column . . . therefore you must not be weak but strong. . . . You are a column, yet of yourself you are weak; but graft yourself onto the tree of the cross, and with affection and boundless, ineffable love bind yourself to the bleeding Lamb. . . . Once the soul has experienced and tasted such sweet love, strong beyond every strength, it can no longer consider nor desire anything else but Him. . . . [29]

How Christians Should Act Toward Bishops

The Fathers of the Church also have much to say on how a bishop should be regarded. To his fellow Christians, Ignatius of Antioch writes: "We should regard the bishop as the Lord himself." [30] And elsewhere he goes on to say:

See that you all follow the bishop, as Jesus Christ follows the Father. . . . Let no one do any of the things appertaining to the Church without the bishop. Let that be considered a valid Eucharist which is celebrated by the bishop, or by one whom he appoints.

Whenever the bishop appears let the congregation be present; just as wherever Jesus Christ is, there is the Catholic Church. It is not lawful either to baptize or to hold an "agape" without the bishop. . . . [31]

He who honors the bishop has been honored by God; he who does anything concealing it from the bishop is serving the devil.[32]

Irenaeus clearly states that "it is necessary to obey the presbyters [bishops]...."[33] And in this regard, Cyprian says: "The heresies have arisen and the schisms have started solely because of the fact that the bishop is not obeyed...."[34]

John Chrysostom poses the question: "Must we obey a superior when he is wicked?" And he gives the following answer:

... if you mean in regard to faith, then indeed flee and avoid him, but if it be in regard to his life ... then listen to Christ who says: "The Scribes and Pharisees sit on Moses' seat" ... and then he says: "... so practice and observe whatever they tell you, but not what they do" (Mt. 23:2-3).[35]

And here as well, Catherine of Siena has words to say that she puts in the mouth of the Eternal Father:

... every homage given to my ministers is not

given to them but to me, because of the blood that I have given them to administer. . . .

. . . my Christs must not be touched by the hands of the laity. No one can excuse himself by saying, "I am doing no wrong . . . to the holy Church, but I am rebelling against the faults of the wicked shepherds." Anyone who says this lies . . . [and] does not see that he is persecuting the blood and not them.

. . . It is I who must punish them; not you. [36]

How the Focolare Movement has Regarded Bishops

At this point it seems both interesting and useful to say something about how the Focolare Movement has regarded bishops in the various moments of its history. Back in 1947 we wrote:

Here is the new Word of Life; "He who hears you hears me" (Lk. 10:16).

Our soul, caught up by the voices of this world, needs so much to hear the voice of Christ! But you must not expect Christ to descend to earth to speak to you. When he was here on earth, he appointed his ministers: those who were to carry on in his place.

Go to them with faith!

You are fighting a battle for the triumph of the spirit over matter, of the supernatural over the natural and the human. . . . Watch out for this blind and deceitful world. Raise yourself up to a purer vision of things. Look at the minister — whoever he is — without regard to his possible faults. His word is the word of God: this is what matters. So do not look at the way in which it is presented to you.

"He who hears you hears me"! Jesus wants to be listened to through his ministers. This is the way he established it; this is the way it is.

And in 1948:

Obedience to authority is necessary even when it seems to us that this authority is not acting in line with our own way of thinking. All that remains for us to do — once we have given our own opinion with detachment — is obey: whether it costs blood, whether it costs our life.

In 1952:

We must neither discuss nor hesitate. We are one only in the Divine Will, and that is expressed by the bishop.

In 1956:

From experience we can say that bishops are different from other people. One senses it when one tells them about our spirituality, or when they speak. Their words have a weight and an unction that immediately distinguishes them from even the holiest priest or theologian. Moreover, they have the grace to get to the point of the matter, and to explain it amply. It is the charism.

In 1958:

In our gatherings when a bishop arrives we feel at home. We feel that someone has come who contains us completely; and we would like to say to him, "Stay with us, for it is near evening."

The Church hierarchy is that channel through which we receive so many graces, and through which God sends his gifts to the whole Church. There are special channels for everyone: for the Florentines, the cardinal of Florence; for others, that of Turin. It is enough to believe that in them is the Church, who is our Mother, and who — as a mother — nourishes us.

In 1960 I said:

I have observed that frequently, even among Catholics, there is something not quite right. We can see that everyone is hungry for truth — people search for it on television, on the radio, in the newspapers — because the soul thirsts for truth.

There is a person on this earth who at times speaks "ex cathedra" and is infallible, and is on very familiar terms with the One who is the Truth: Christ. And there are the bishops who, under certain conditions, are also infallible because they are vicars of Christ. They speak; but few newspapers report what they have said, and very few read it.

I wish that everyone would feel that they have a mother, and that this mother is always there to nourish them. And I wish that everyone would seek this genuine milk, which is given by the Holy Father and the bishops; and that they would drink it and make it their own.

I assure you that they would experience what we have experienced. The more we have Jesus present in our midst, through this Ideal we live, the more we understand the beauty of what the Church hierarchy tells us.

It is logical! Because Christ is the Spouse of the Church.

The Church is the spouse of Christ.

Where Christ is, there is the Church.

Where the Church is, there is Christ.

In short, I wish that everyone had this hunger in his soul!

And again in 1960:

I acknowledge now, looking back, that our living these words "He who hears you hears me" deeply, profoundly, and generously, has been one of the most effective causes of the explosive spreading of the Movement.

Truly, whoever remains united to him through the hierarchy, bears abundant fruit.

In 1961:

The other day Fr. Foresi spoke to us of the various charisms that a soul can possess. But can you imagine what it would be like if everyone were pushing the importance of their own charism? Instead of a concert we would have chaos. . . . There is a need in the Church for a charism which gives order to all these charisms.

And this is the charism that we have found —
not only through faith, but through experience
— in our superiors.

Again in 1961:

In order to see how we ought to behave
towards our superiors, let us look to Mary. She
is the model of the Christian.

At the wedding feast at Cana she risks making
a comment to Jesus. (And as we know, Our
Lady is perfect, and she listens to the Holy
Spirit.) She goes to Jesus and says, "they have
no more wine"; but Jesus replies, "What do you
want of me, woman?" And Our Lady then
surrenders her idea, saying to the servants, "Do
whatever he tells you." But because she has
given up her idea, Jesus makes it his own, and
changes the water into wine (Cf. Jn. 2:3-10).

And yet again, in 1961:

In our superiors we must see Jesus; but not
merely as we would in any neighbor. We owe
them not only our love, not only our life, but
total obedience — which signifies even giving up

something which at times could be worth more than life itself. For example, if they should say to us that our Movement is not right, we would have to obey.

This unity with the hierarchy must remain one of our fundamental characteristics.

In 1969:

We frequently affirm that we have lived the words "He who hears you hears me"; and we sincerely say that we were ready to renounce all that we thought, if the Church had not approved it. Now I see that this was not only out of principle — obedience to the Church — or simply from fear of heresy; it was actually the Church which was drawing us to itself. Or better still, it was the Holy Spirit in us who urged us to be united with the Holy Spirit who is in the Church, because it is one and the same Holy Spirit.

The Bishop as Seen by Vatican II

If — after all that has been said — we now cite a few passages from the documents of the Second Vatican Council, we will be able to appreciate more fully how much the Catholic Church has always been in harmony with the scriptures and with tradition; and we will enrich our own understanding of the bishops as well.

In *Lumen Gentium* (Latin: "Light of the nations"), the Council's Constitution on the Church, we find the following statements:

> With their helpers, the priests and deacons, bishops have therefore taken up the service of the community, presiding in place of God over the flock whose shepherds they are, as teachers of doctrine, priests of sacred worship, and officers of good order. Just as the role that the Lord gave individually to Peter . . . is permanent . . . so also the apostle's office . . . is permanent, and was meant to be exercised without interruption by the sacred order of bishops. . . . By divine institution bishops have succeeded to the place of the apostles as shepherds of the Church. . . . [37]

Every legitimate celebration of the Eucharist is regulated by the bishop, to whom is committed the office of offering the worship of Christian religion . . . and of administering it in accordance with the Lord's commandments and with the Church's laws. . . .

. . . Finally, by the example of their manner of life, the Bishops must be an influence for good on those over whom they preside, by refraining from all evil. . . . [38]

Bishops govern the particular churches entrusted to them as the vicars and ambassadors of Christ. This they do by their counsel, exhortations, and example, as well, indeed, as by their authority and sacred power. This power they use only for the edification of their flock in truth and holiness, remembering that he who is greater should become as the lesser and he who is the more distinguished, as the servant (Cf. Lk. 22:26-27). . . . This power . . . is proper, ordinary, and immediate, although its exercise is ultimately regulated by the supreme authority of the Church. . . . In virtue of this power, bishops have the sacred right and the duty . . . to make laws for their subjects, to pass judgment on them, and to moderate everything pertaining to the ordering of worship and the apostolate.

... himself beset with weakness, [the bishop] is able to have compassion on the ignorant and erring (Cf. Heb. 5:1-2). Let him not refuse to listen to his subjects, whom he cherishes as his true children and exhorts to cooperate readily with him. As having one day to render to God an account for their souls (Cf. Heb. 13:17), he takes care of them by his prayer, preaching, and all the works of charity, and not only of them, but also of those who are not yet of the one flock. For these also are commended to him in the Lord. [39]

In this regard, G. Philips comments:

How should the instruction given to the Church's superiors to "listen" to their subjects be interpreted? ... [In this way:] that the subjects of the bishop are his true sons and daughters, and he calls them to work with him — not as servants, but as collaborators, in the literal sense of the word.... But there is something more. The bishop himself must also listen to the word of God. Now, this often comes to him from the lips of a subordinate;

but, in reality, it is from the Holy Spirit. Or should we consider the paragraphs [of Vatican II] on charisms as literature without meaning?[40]

Let us conclude with the words of Pope Paul VI:

The bishops are placed by the Holy Spirit to nourish the Church of God. "To nourish": a decisive word which . . . marvelously fuses the juridical charism of authority with the sovereign charism of love. . . .[41]

4.

The One Who Loves Most

Whenever I have had an audience with Pope Paul VI, I have felt myself face to face with a person who loved in a very special way. This was especially true the first time. The Pope spoke words of wisdom which went beyond all the juridical obstacles which still existed. He understood. And he opened his soul to receive the entire complex Movement which I was presenting to him. He himself encouraged me to tell him everything, because − he assured me − "here, everything is possible".

I remember that I felt a perfect harmony between what the Pope was saying to me and what I felt had come from God for the building up of this Movement. It was such a strong impression, that it almost seemed that the study where the Pope receives his guests had no ceiling, and that there heaven and earth met. If I had been taken before him blindfolded, and had never before heard his voice, after a time I think that I would have affirmed, "I am with the Pope."

Paul VI does great honor to the papacy. He is not afraid to love everyone, and so he already creates a certain unity among believers and non-believers. He gives himself to all in a striking manner. Very many Christians of the most varied denominations have been extremely impressed by the person of the Pope, by the love which consumes him, by his making himself — as the Apostle says — "all things to all men." Perhaps this is one of the reasons why Patriarch Athenagoras called him Paul II. And it has given these non-Catholic visitors a special esteem for him.

Moreover, with this attitude of his, Paul VI reveals the program of his pontificate: he is the Pope who dialogues with the whole world; he is the Pope who sees all of mankind as potentially one family, one single nation.

The Pope is alone in his responsibility, which embraces the world; nor could he share his mission in its entirety with another person. For he would be disturbed in listening to the voice of the Holy Spirit who speaks in him in a unique manner.

But Mary is there: she is the one who sustains the popes. Between Paul VI — who proclaimed the Mother of God to be Mother of the Church — and Mary there is a unique and profound rapport, inaccessible to any other member of the faithful.

The Pope and the Primacy in the Course of History

Let us look briefly at the figure of the pope and his position of primacy among the bishops in the post-apostolic age. *The Episcopal Ministry,* the ecumenical document of the Group of Dombes, says:

. . . for the churches of the apostolic age, even after the passing of the initial college, the person of Peter in the midst of the twelve is a sign of the union of the *episcope* and a symbol of its ministry (Mt. 16:18-19; Lk. 22:32; Gal. 1:18).[1]

About the year 107, Ignatius, the second bishop of Antioch, wrote a splendid letter to the Romans which interests us because of the recognition that it contains of the primacy of the Church of Rome. Right from the initial greeting, it is quite different in tone from the letters which Ignatius addresses to the other churches to whom he writes.

Ignatius . . . to the church . . . which presides

in the place of the country of the Romans, worthy of God, worthy of honor and blessing, worthy of praise and success, worthy in its holiness, and which presides over love, true to Christ's law . . . I greet you. . . .[2]

Ignatius says that the Church of Rome is the one which "presides over love." The term *prokatemene* ("who presides over") always contains an idea of authority. The term *agape* ("love") is sometimes used by Ignatius as a synonym for the local church;[3] but here it could mean the totality of the supernatural life enkindled by Jesus.[4] This greeting, observes Quasten, the noted authority on the Fathers of the Church, "is the earliest avowal of the primacy of Rome that we possess from the pen of a non-Roman ecclesiastic."[5] And he concludes:

But, aside from the problem presented by so difficult an expression ["who presides over"], the Epistle to the Romans, taken in its entirety, shows beyond cavil that the position of honor accorded the Roman Church is acknowledged by Ignatius as her due, and is founded . . . on her inherent right to universal ecclesiastical supremacy.[6]

From the same letter one can also deduce that the Roman Church had already exercised its doctrinal authority. For Ignatius affirms: "You have been others' teachers."[7]

Moreover, Ignatius does not dare to admonish the Church of Rome as he does the other churches, because it derives its authority from the apostles Peter and Paul, who lived there and who announced the Gospel there.[8] This is the most important reason for the supremacy of the Church of Rome.

In the year 96, Pope Clement of Rome, writing in the name of the Roman Church, sent a lengthy letter to the Corinthians which has since been referred to as "the epiphany of the Roman primacy."[9] In this letter, Clement gives precise orders to the Corinthians, which clearly reveals his authority:

> . . . we view it as a breach of justice to remove from their ministry those who were appointed by [the apostles] or later on . . . by others of proper standing. . . .[10]
> . . . it is disgraceful . . . to have it reported that because of one or two individuals the solid and ancient Corinthian Church is in revolt against its presbyters [bishops].[11]

. . . You who are responsible for the revolt must submit to the presbyters [bishops].[12]

If, on the other hand, there be some who fail to obey . . . they must realize that they will enmesh themselves in sin and in no insignificant danger.[13]

You will make us exceedingly happy if you prove obedient to what we, prompted by the Holy Spirit, have written, and if, following the plea of our letter for peace and harmony, you rid yourselves of your wicked and passionate rivalry.

We are sending you, moreover, trustworthy and discreet persons who from youth to old age have lived irreproachable lives among us. They will be witnesses to mediate between us.[14]

Writing toward the end of the second century, Irenaeus draws our attention to the importance of the Church of Rome:

. . . But since it would be very long . . . to enumerate the successions of all the churches, I can [point out] the tradition which that very great, oldest, and well-known church, founded and established at Rome by those two most glorious apostles Peter and Paul, received from the apostles, and its faith known among men, which comes down to us through the succession of bishops. . . . For every church must be [doctrinally] in harmony with this church because of its outstanding pre-eminence. . . . [15]

Tertullian, almost a contemporary of Irenaeus, exclaims his admiration for the Roman Church in these words:

How blessed is this Church [of Rome]! It was the apostles themselves, in shedding their blood, who poured out on her the doctrine in its entirety. It is the church where Peter was made equal to the Lord in his passion; where Paul was crowned with the martyrdom of John [the Baptist]; where the apostle John was immersed in boiling oil, only to emerge unharmed and then be banished to an island. We can see then, what this church has learned, what it has taught, and what it bears witness to. . . . [16]

And Cyprian, who lived from 210 to 258, and is noted for the importance he assigns to the episcopate, states: "God is one, Christ is one, the Church is one; and one is the chair founded on

Peter by the Lord's words." [17]   And elsewhere he
writes:

The Lord says to Peter: "I tell you, you are
Peter . . . I will give you the keys of the kingdom
of heaven" (Mt. 16:18-19).
. . . And after the resurrection he says to him:
"Feed my sheep" (Jn. 21:17). [Jesus] builds the
Church on one person alone, and commands him
to feed his sheep. And although he gives all the
apostles equal power, nevertheless he establishes
only one chair; and with the authority of his
word he establishes the origin of unity.
The other apostles were certainly everything
that Peter was, but the primacy was given to
Peter so that the Church would visibly be one,
and the chair one.
. . . Can anyone who abandons the chair of
Peter, on which the Church is founded, still
think that he is in the Church?[18]

With regard to the East — though this is not the
moment to take up the difficult question of the
Eastern Churches — we can nevertheless affirm
that:

St. Gregory of Nyssa, St. Gregory of Nazianzen, Eusebius of Caesarea and St. John Chrysostom understand Mt. 16:18 ["And I tell you, you are Peter, and on this rock I will build my Church, and the powers of death shall not prevail against it."] to mean the primacy of Peter. A certain number [of Greek Fathers of the Church], accepting the consequences of this, give witness to their own faith in the primacy of Peter's successors in Rome. Gregory of Nazianzen says that the Roman Church "presides over . . . the whole world." [19,20]

And John Chrysostom writes that Christ "shed his blood to redeem the sheep that he entrusted to Peter and to his successors."[21] And it is beautiful to see how he describes his love for Rome:

I esteem it blessed because Paul . . . wrote to its citizens and loved them intensely, and he spoke with them personally, and ended his life there. . . . Just think of the awesome sight that Rome will behold when Paul suddenly rises from the tomb, together with Peter, and goes forth to meet the Lord! . . . This is why I admire this city — not for the gold, not for the statues, not for all its pomp, but for these two pillars of the Church. [22]

It is evident, therefore, that the veneration and admiration which Christian Rome inspires are firmly rooted far back in history.

Peter's Succession

If — as we have seen — it was necessary for the apostles to appoint successors to carry on their mission of bringing the Gospel to the ends of the earth, it was all the more necessary that someone continue that special function which Peter had had as head of the apostolic college. For if Jesus, while he himself was still on earth, appointed Peter as head of the apostolic college, then the college of bishops — the apostles' successors — would have all the more reason to need a bishop who, as Peter's successor, would guarantee its unity down through the centuries. In fact, in the fourth century we find Augustine writing:

For if the order of succession of bishops is to be considered, how much more surely, truly and safely do we number them from Peter, to whom, as representing the whole Church, the Lord said: "Upon this rock I will build my Church . . ." (Mt. 16:18). For, to Peter succeeded Linus, to Linus Clement, to Clement Anacletus, to Anacletus Evaristus, to Evaristus Sixtus, to Sixtus Telesphorus, to Telesphorus Hyginus . . . [23]

And he goes on to list all Peter's successors down to Anastasius, the pope at that time.

Pope Innocent I — Anastasius' successor — had no doubts about the primacy, as he wrote to the bishops gathered at the Council of Carthage, among whom was Augustine himself.

In searching for solutions to theological questions . . . you have kept the precedents of ancient tradition and the norms of ecclesiastical discipline. In doing so you have truly added to the strength of our religion: first by formulating your decrees, and now as well, by asking our opinion, because you have acknowledged it your duty to submit them to our judgment, knowing well what is due to the Apostolic See, in which all of us who occupy this position, wish to follow the Apostle himself, from whom the episcopate itself is derived, as well as the authority of all the bishops. [24]

In the fifth century, Leo the Great spoke very clearly regarding the primacy: he proved it theologically and he defended it. In the "Fourth Sermon" he says:

... [Peter] was filled by the source itself of all charisms with such an abundance, that without his mediation nothing can pass to anyone else, although many gifts were given to him personally.... In the whole world, Peter alone is chosen ... to preside over all the apostles ... so that in spite of the fact that there are many priests and many pastors among the people of God, Peter truly governs over all [in subordination] to Christ.... [25]

... the Lord said, "[Simon] I have prayed for you, that your faith may not fail; and when you have turned again, strengthen your brothers" (Lk. 22:31-32.).... The Lord ... prayed particularly for Peter's faith.... Therefore, everyone's strength is defended in Peter.... The steadfastness which Christ conceded to Peter is transmitted through Peter to the [other] apostles. [26]

And in the "Fifth Sermon":

The Blessed Peter . . . continues to be the head of his see and to have an immortal communion with the eternal Priest. The firmness which Peter received from Christ, by whom he was appointed, is also transmitted to his heirs. . . .[27]

In his commentary on the Second Vatican Council, Gerard Philips makes the following statement in reference to the primacy:

There is no stronger defender of the Roman primacy than Pope Leo the Great: We bear the concern of all the churches, he wrote to the bishops of Illyria . . . and we share this solicitude with all those who are united to us "in the charity of this college." [28, 29]

Living at the end of the sixth century, Gregory the Great — first pope to refer to himself in his letters as the "servant of the servants of God" — strongly believed in Leo the Great's conception of the primacy of Rome: that is, that the bishop of Rome has the right and the duty to guide the universal Church. Being an outstanding person of great holiness, and given the historical situation, he was able to greatly strengthen the position of the papacy, especially in the West.

The Church in the Following Centuries

After all that has been mentioned above, the history of the Church has unfolded through the centuries amidst painful divisions between Christians; sad and tragic times; enlightened reforms; the works and triumphs of countless saints; the foundations of fruitful orders and congregations — which have made the Church a magnificent garden: full of flower beds perfumed with the scent of the Gospel's words and illustrating and honoring the life of Jesus in all its various moments; and an ever greater expansion. Those Christians with whom the bond of unity had been weakened, due to a lack of Christian charity on both sides, organized themselves into churches and ecclesial communities by the hundreds.

From time to time the Catholic Church has needed to meet in Councils, which have decreed whatever the Holy Spirit and the college of bishops together with the pope, have considered is for the good of the Church. Recently, dogmas concerning the Blessed Virgin have been proclaimed, and she is known and venerated more and more.

While this might seem to many to be a course of action counter-productive to the cause of unification, perhaps — after so many centuries of struggle between Christians — it is Mary herself who is enkindling in the hearts of the Catholic faithful an unprecedented love towards their other brothers and sisters. And at the same time, the Holy Spirit, together with Mary who is mother of all, has brought about a flourishing ecumenical movement, towards which hardly a single church or ecclesial community has remained indifferent. And so in our own time love is blossoming, pushing aside the polemics of the past. And Jesus' prayer for the unity of Christians has become the prayer of this century.

The Pope

In this journey of all toward unity — long and demanding, but rich in true hope — the great and universally respected figure of the present Pope stands out, reminding us of all the saintly popes who have preceded him, and of the many saints who have kept alive through the centuries the true image of the pope.

Catherine of Siena, Doctor of the Church, said to Jesus: "When you left us, you did not leave us orphans, but you left us your vicar who baptizes us with the Holy Spirit."[30] And in her *Dialogue* the Eternal Father says:

> To whom did I leave the keys of this blood? To the glorious apostle Peter and to all the others who have come and who will come after him, until the day of the Last Judgment. They have and will continue to have the very same authority which Peter had, and none of their faults will ever diminish this authority, or ever take away from the blood or any of the sacraments their perfection. [31]

The Pope's Role Seen from the Pope's Point of View

No one can say who the Pope is better than the Pope himself. During a general audience in 1964, Paul VI posed this question: "Who is the Pope?"

And went on to explain:

> ... [The Lord] himself wanted to define the person of the one he was choosing as the first of his disciples. . . . He would no longer be called Simon, . . . his name at birth, but Peter, the name of his office. Here it is evident that Jesus was giving his chosen one a special virtue and a special office, both represented by the image of the stone, the rock: that is the virtue of firmness, of stability, of solidity, of immobility, of persevering unfailingly amidst the passage of time and the hardships of life; and the office of acting as the foundation, the cornerstone, the support, as Jesus himself said to Peter at the Last Supper: "Strengthen your brothers" (Lk. 22:32*).
>
> The Lord's intentions are very clear, and this is what makes the papacy unique and marvelous . . . a miracle of equilibrium, resistance, and vitality, that finds its explanation in the presence of Christ in the person of Peter! [32]

Speaking of his role to twenty thousand faithful at Bombay in 1964, the Pope said:

> If you ask, "Who is this pilgrim?" . . . we will answer that we are the servant and messenger of Jesus Christ, placed by divine Providence at the

head of his Church as successor of St. Peter, Prince of the Apostles. To be the messenger of Jesus and head of the Church are in reality one function, since the very reason for the Church's existence is to proclaim and spread the teaching of Jesus and to continue his ministry on earth. This is our identity and our mission.[33]

The question, "Do you love me more than these?" (Jn. 21:15), which Jesus asked Peter, is a constant source of torment and reflection for Paul VI. He himself has said this time and again during public audiences as well as on other occasions. During a general audience in 1965 he said:

... The secret of our personal comfort as well as our personal torment is contained and expressed in one simple but awe-inspiring syllable that is pronounced "more," *"plus,"* *"pleon"* (Jn. 21:15), which Jesus united in a very unexpected but luminous way, to the verb "love." ... Together with this primacy of authority ... Jesus desires a corresponding primacy of love. The former [authority] is a totally gratuitous power; the latter [love] is a virtue in which a great gift, a great grace, a great capacity of loving must blend with the greatest effort, the greatest impetus of the human heart called to such heights of love. [34]

And yet again he says:

One has to be in the Pope's place to understand how that little phrase: "Do you love me more?" is a knife that penetrates to the joints, the nerves, to the very marrow. . . . How can one know if one loves *more?* . . . What gives comfort in this torment is that one can love universally . . . and repeat: no one is a stranger to me, no one is excluded — no one, even though separated or far away. Every person loved is present.[35]

Now there can be no further doubts. The greatest heart on earth, the one most open and most generous, the one most similar to the heart of Christ is the heart of the Pope. This miracle is and will continue to be brought about by Jesus' words, "Do you love me more than these?" (Jn. 21:15). This heart is worthy to feed the Church because, just as a mother carries her child in her womb, the Pope carries humanity in his heart.

111

And what better place for us the faithful to be than in that heart!

5.

Powers and Service

The Church is not as beautiful as it could be! And we the faithful are to blame, for our lack of fidelity to the Church and to those who represent it: the Pope and the bishops.

But that passionate love for the Church which the Holy Father once spoke about, must invade our hearts and help us to understand why the Church is not as it could be. Then our hearts will be filled with such enthusiasm, and our minds with such light, that we will be able to shake ourselves out of our apathy, and motivate ourselves and others to renew the Church, which now seems less beautiful due to the lack of love, the little faith, and the great ignorance of those who are baptized.

The Church as It Could Be

When, some time ago, I read some statements of Ignatius of Antioch, my heart jumped for joy. There I found words that only the Holy Spirit could have dictated. There I found the Church as it should be. Writing to the Ephesians, Ignatius says:

> Therefore it is fitting that you should live in harmony with the mind of the bishop, as indeed you do. For your rightly famous presbytery [council of presbyters (priests) around the bishop], worthy of God, is harmoniously united to the bishop as the strings to the harp. Therefore, by your accord and harmonious love you sing Jesus Christ.[1]

This is splendid! It seems like poetry, but instead it is simply an expression of the way the Church is meant to be. Someone might be tempted to interpret it superficially, but it is most profound. Just think: the faithful, and particularly the presbyters, are united to the bishop like the strings to the harp.

What does this mean? It means that in Ignatius' time, there was a much more vital awareness than there is now of who the bishop is: that the bishop — as Ignatius defines him — is the one who presides "in the place of God." Well then, how would the faithful who possess this faith behave toward the bishop? Just as they would behave if they were dealing with Jesus Christ himself: they would open their hearts and minds, and put aside their own interests and concerns, in order to hear and to receive what Jesus is telling them in the bishop. Then, inspired by Jesus, the bishop would open his mouth and — not finding any obstacles in his path, but only love — would express himself fully, with that wisdom which captivates us, spurs us on, and enables us to do great things.

Moreover, through the unity of the faithful with the bishop, as the strings to the harp, Christ would also be present in a new way, since he is there wherever two or more are united in his name. And this presence would give the words of the bishop further unction, light, persuasiveness and strength, so as to make all even more one in God. And through Christ present in the bishop and among them, all would "sing Jesus Christ"; that is, the reality of Christ would be mirrored in a living Church.

If then — since the Holy Spirit is given to all the faithful — someone feels that he has received some direction or inspiration from the Lord, and therefore has something he must tell the bishop, how should he go about it? Acting out of love and with detachment, he should *give* what he feels to the bishop; and Jesus in the bishop will then be able to speak freely, uttering words in harmony with what this person feels deep within him. The results will be a further confirmation of that Christian's faith that it is Christ who speaks in the bishop, and that by doing what the bishop says, one is doing what God wants.

But this is not the only thing Ignatius says; he adds:

> And each one must become part of this choir, so that in perfect harmony, and taking your pitch from God in unison, you may sing with one voice to the Father through Jesus Christ. Then he will both hear you and recognize by your good works that you are members of his Son. Therefore it is important that you always be in irreproachable unity, in order that you may always be in union with God.[2]

Certainly, in order for the Church to be as it should be, each member of the faithful must also "become part of this choir," and this is accomplished by living with the others in one accord of mind and heart. Then, presupposing that there is unity with the hierarchy, this fraternal unity brings about the presence of Jesus "where two or three are gathered" in his name. And since Jesus is there, the Church is there, as in the famous phrase of Tertullian: "Where three [are gathered . . .] even lay people, there is the Church."[3] And in this way we can take our "pitch from God in unison," as Ignatius says, and "sing with one voice to the Father through Jesus Christ," who is there among all and in all.

Now, the Christian community as Ignatius conceived it — unity with the bishop, and above all with the pope; and unity among the faithful — is certainly possible, and anything but passive.

We must hope that, even though the weeds cannot be rooted out from the good grain, the faithful in the Church, even in the farthest corners of the earth, will hear the call of Jesus to unity, so that the Spouse of Christ might be fully alive with his life, and fully a witness to God.

Besides, ours is the age of unity. The Holy Spirit is breathing this word and giving life to this reality at various levels within the Church: in the Ecumenical Council; in the Pope, who so often extolls unity, the first mark of the Church; and in various spiritual movements.

Having made this introduction, let us continue

our study of Christ's presence in the hierarchy, an essential premise for a renewal of the Church in unity. We shall be guided by the light of the Scriptures and the words of the Pope, with the help of various theologians.

Jesus in the Hierarchy: Head of His Body the Church

In the Church, which is his Mystical Body, Jesus is the Head. Paul explains this to the Colossians: "[Christ is] the Head, from whom the whole body, nourished and knit together ... grows ..." (Col. 2:19); and he repeats it to the Ephesians: ". . . speaking the truth in love, we are to grow up in every way into him who is the head, into Christ, from whom the whole body . . . makes bodily growth and builds itself up in love" (Eph. 4:15-16).

But Jesus has transmitted his role as head to the apostles, so that they might pasture the flock which has been entrusted to them. He said, in fact: "As the Father has sent me, even so I send you" (Jn. 20:21). And he meant: as the Father wanted me Head of the Church, so I want you; and this is how I am sending you out. [4]

120

The historical Jesus, in fact, was to rise from the dead and to ascend beyond time and space to the right hand of the Father, distinct from his Body the Church. From heaven he would continue to keep his Church in existence, to nourish her, to guide her, and to maintain her in unity, through the hierarchy, which would carry out the functions of Christ, Head of the Church. Journet says that as its head, Christ maintains contact with his body, the Church, through the hierarchy.[5]

We could cite many authoritative sources in support of this view on authority in the Church. We particularly like those of Paul VI and the theologians Marranzini and O'Connor. Paul VI teaches:

> The authority in the Church ... did not establish itself, but it was instituted by Christ; it was his idea, his will. And so in dealing with the authority of the Church, we must feel that we are in the presence of Christ. "He who hears you hears me" (Lk. 10:16), the Lord said. And every time that an attempt is made to contest this institution ... one goes against the word, the plan, the love of Christ.[6]

Moreover, Marranzini writes: "Everyone in the Church, even those with the greatest charisms, are bound to submit themselves to Christ in the person of his ordained ministers."[7] And O'Connor, in his study, "Charisme et Institution", says:

For the Prince of Shepherds (1 Pt. 5:4) has not dismissed his flock for them to be led through the desert by guides not always trustworthy. He himself continues to conduct his People, and he does this by means of those appointed to represent him, and in spite of their flaws.[8]

The Hierarchy and the Focolare Movement

Since this is a matter which involves all the faithful, let us see what sort of experience the Focolare Movement has had in dealing with the hierarchy of the Church.

We did not need to study at length in order to know whether or not Christ was present in the hierarchy which descends from Peter and the apostles. The truth contained in the words of the Gospel, "He who hears you hears me . . ." (Lk.

10:16) brought light to our hearts and minds, and that was enough. And now, alongside its faith in the presence of Christ in the hierarchy as understood by the Magisterium of the Church, the Movement also has a very valuable treasure to offer: its thirty-five years of experience.

We can say, in all conscience, that always, always, on occasions too numerous to count, we have found God in the hierarchy. This has been so in every instance: whether the hierarchy was confirming our ideas; whether it was causing our hearts to be filled with joy at its teachings, its approvals, and its encouragements; or whether God was using it to correct us and help us to become better. For those in the Movement, the truth that Jesus is present in the hierarchy has been so thoroughly verified through experience, that we joyfully and easily believe it.

The Bishops and the People of God

We have already said that by the laying on of hands, the apostles ordained other worthy men to be their successors, and passed on to them the life that Christ had transmitted to them. The very same thing was done by the successors of the apostles with their own successors, maintaining in this way the "apostolic succession," which has continued down to the present. Therefore, as we are already well aware, the bishops of the Church are vitally united to Christ.

These bishops are gifts of God to the Church, because as a sacrament (visible sign) of Christ the Head, they generate the Church down through the centuries. Viewing them in this perspective, one would have to say that since the bishops share Christ's paternal role toward his Body the Church, they — the hierarchy — come *before* the Church.

But it is also true that the Church comes before the hierarchy, as Congar says: "The first priority . . . is the formation of a communion of the faithful, in the midst of which the Lord stirs up gifts and forms of service through which he builds up his body."[9]

For this reason the Council dealt first with the People of God, which includes both the faithful and the hierarchy, and then dealt with the hierarchy.

Spirit and Structure in the Church

Having spoken thus far of the hierarchy of the Church and of the role of authority in the Church, it is evident to us that the Christian community as Christ wanted it is not only a communion in love, but also a community, guided, supported, vivified, and nourished by the hierarchical structure.

In answer to those who assert that "the ills which the Church suffers from are caused by its being 'too juridical,'" Paul VI said that "just as the soul cannot be separated from the body without this resulting in the death of the body itself, likewise the Church which calls itself 'charity,' 'love,' cannot exist without the 'juridical' Church." [10]

Gerard Philips writes: "The community as Christ wanted it, necessarily involves a hierarchy of powers, in which the superior guides the subordinate." [11] For many today, these words sound too strong, anachronistic and medieval. In this age in which we live, characterized by protests against all structures, there is such a love of freedom that at times it even leads some people into anarchy. And there are those who would throw off all rules and any sort of good order as willingly as they would a heavy suit of armor.

Naturally enough, the religious sphere has not remained unaffected by what is happening in the secular world; all the more so since atheism, immorality and indifference have extinguished the faith in many and destroyed the appeal of Christian virtue.

The most that is accepted of the Gospel message is the concept of love towards one's neighbor. But what is not understood are the other virtues which Jesus lived in such a heroic and exemplary way, and with which his entire life is interwoven: obedience, mortification, meekness, purity, patience, temperance, and love for the cross. For many today, these are nothing more than foolish ideas, still considered worthwhile only by groups of senile old people who do not love life.

For this reason, the Christian world urgently needs a revolution, a renewal whose roots are founded in the true Christ.

Gerard Philips stated that in the Church "the superior guides the subordinate." It is not difficult, therefore, to understand the Pope and to accept his idea as our own when he says: "The Church needs obedience." The Pope points out that there is still a need today to talk about obedience, since a certain dissatisfaction still surfaces here and there.

[The need] persists because of the increased necessity in this post-conciliar period for internal cohesion [in the Church] . . . how can we renew the spirit, the works, and the structures of the Church, if there is not solidarity within the Church itself? How can we approach our separated brothers and sisters . . .? And how can we speak to the world that we would like to evangelize, if among us the wisdom and authority to do so has been weakened, due to a lack of that apostolic authenticity, which obedience alone qualifies and gives life to?

. . . Has there been some change in obedience with the Council? Oh, no! . . . even before being a purely formal and juridical observing of Church laws and submission to Church authority, obedience is the penetration and acceptance of the mystery of Christ, who saved us through obedience . . . it is the understanding of the principle which dominates the whole plan of the Incarnation and the Redemption. . . .[12]

[With the Council] we note that, without excluding the elements of responsibility and decision making reserved to those in authority, the concept of such a relationship [of authority and obedience] has been enriched with elements now much more valued, such as respect, trust, unity, collaboration, co-responsibility, kindness, friendship, love . . . which bring it back to its evangelical content . . .[13]

Yes, obedience does seem new after the Second Vatican Council precisely because of this collaboration, co-responsibility, and friendship, which facilitate the unity between the superior and the subordinate. And in unity, obedience loses that element of separation or distance, because in collaborating, in loving a friend, one obeys almost without noticing it.

The Function of Bishops

Let us now see how Jesus is present in the hierarchy. Paul has taught us that Jesus is present in the Church as its head. Reading over what Jesus says of himself, we can understand the full meaning of this word "head." Jesus says: "I am the Way, the Truth and the Life" (Jn. 14:6); and he admits before Pilate that he is a king (cf. Lk. 23:3).

He calls himself "the good shepherd" (Jn. 10:11); and affirms that there is "only one teacher, the Christ" (Mt. 23:10*). He is the Prophet above all others, not only because he speaks in the name of God, but because he is the very Word of God; he is the Word Incarnate. He is pleased when Peter calls him "the Christ" ("the Anointed One", "the Messiah") and "the Son of God" (Mt. 16:16); that is, *the* Saint in the fullest sense of the word. John the Baptist calls him "the Lamb of God" (Jn. 1:29), that is "victim"; and his very name "Jesus" signifies "God saves," the Savior.

Everything which Jesus, the Head, says of himself, the bishops can say of Jesus acting in them. In this way we see three principal roles emerging: the pastoral or governing role, in which Jesus acts in his ministers more as a shepherd, as a king, as the Way; the teaching or prophetic role, in which Jesus acts more as a teacher, as a prophet, as the Truth; and finally, the sacramental, sanctifying role, in which Jesus acts as priest, as victim: the Lamb of God, as Savior, as the Life.

These are three aspects of the function of Christ, the Head, in his ministers; aspects which, even though they can be distinguished, actually permeate one another. In governing and in teaching, Jesus is present and acts in his ministers using their human capacities; and so it may be that one bishop has a more learned approach than another in expounding a particular truth. In the sacramental role, instead, Jesus present in his ministers acts independently of their human capacities, so that in every Mass — for example — whether celebrated by a highly educated bishop or one less so, the very same mystery of the Eucharist is fulfilled; and the same applies for the other sacraments.

Let us now examine these roles, one by one, in order to better understand the dynamics of the life of Christ in his ministers.

The Kingly or Pastoral Role

What is the purpose of the governing role which Jesus entrusted to the hierarchy? Paul tells us it is ". . . to equip the saints for the work of ministry . . ." (Eph. 4:12); that is, for their role in the Church. For the community of the faithful is not a passive multitude in the hands of a priestly elite. In the body of Christ each member has his role.. The hierarchy, therefore, is the vital organization of the Church which assures each member not only his place, but his role in the Church as a whole.[14]

A further role of government in the Church is to ensure the cohesion of the Body of Christ; that is, to safeguard its unity. And in his letter to the Colossians, Paul compares the ministers to "joints" and "ligaments" (Col. 2:19).

But the image of a shepherd is perhaps that which best defines their mission. To the Twelve Jesus had said: "If a man has a hundred sheep and one of them has gone astray, does he not leave the ninety-nine on the mountains to go in search of the one that went astray?" (Mt. 18:12); and to Peter he said, "Feed my lambs," "feed my sheep" (Jn. 21:15, 16).

Another name, likewise rooted in revelation, which can be appropriately applied to the hierarchy is "mother." For the hierarchy mirrors Christ, who reached his highest expression in his cry of abandonment: "My God, my God, why have you forsaken me?" (Mt. 27:46*). This cry is nothing other than an expression of the pangs of labor of the divine birth of the human race as children of God. In this cry is the birth of the Church.

To see in the hierarchy an expression of the

Church as mother has been one of the strongest experiences of the Focolare Movement. For many years we have had the heartfelt conviction that the Church in the person of its representative is our mother. And it is this conviction which gave confidence, security and strength to the members of the Movement, making it possible for the Movement to spread even while the Church had it under examination. Certainly the image of a shepherd portrays Jesus very well; and, therefore, his ministers must fit this image. But the shepherds which Jesus speaks about are those who give their lives for their sheep; they are not hired hands. They are, therefore, like mothers. A mother does exactly what the Church is doing through its hierarchy: instructing, feeding, guiding, and serving in love.

Authority as Service

Jesus envisions authority in a way which is all his own. Indeed, he views authority as service, thereby overturning the world's way of thinking, and transforming the very nature of authority itself.[15] In Mark's Gospel he says:

You know that those who are supposed to rule over the Gentiles lord it over them, and their great men exercise authority over them. But it shall not be so among you; but whoever would be great among you must be your servant, and whoever would be first among you must be slave of all. For the son of Man also came not to be served but to serve, and to give his life as a ransom for many (Mk. 10:42-45).

In Luke's Gospel, Jesus expresses his thinking with clear reference to those who govern: ". . . let the greatest among you become as the youngest, and the leader as one who serves" (Lk. 22:26). And this is reaffirmed by Paul when he writes to the Corinthians: "[We are] your servants for Jesus' sake" (2 Cor. 4:5). And again: "For though I am not a slave of any man, I have made myself a slave to all, that I might win over as many as possible" (1 Cor. 9:19*).

Peter extends this concept beyond the hierarchy to include all those who have received any charism from God: ". . . put your gifts at the service of one another, each in the measure he has received" (1 Pt. 4:10*).

Authority in the Church, therefore, is not

domination but service. Jesus has inaugurated a new way; and as Congar says, "The disciples cannot rise except by lowering themselves."[16] But with reference to this service, Paul VI makes a point which is quite important:

What type of service is required of one who is vested with the office of guiding and directing? Should this service be subordinate to those who are served, and must it be accountable to them? No, it is a service in the interest of one's brothers, but not subject to them. It is an office of service to which Christ did not entrust an implement of servitude, but rather a sign of ownership, the keys; that is, the powers of the Kingdom of Heaven. It is a service which is accountable to God alone. As St. Paul says of himself: "Qui autem iudicat me, Dominus est" —"It is the Lord who judges me" (1 Cor. 4:4).[17]

What Laberthonniere says is also very beautiful: "The general exercise of authority is but one of the ways in which we must act ... for one another in view of our common destiny."[18] In so saying, while retaining the function of the hierarchy, he gives the Church the features of a community of love, as it will be in heaven. And with the accent on the hierarchy's characteristic of service, the Church-as-institution and the Church-as-community appear more clearly as a unified whole.

Acting as a servant comes so naturally to Jesus, that in announcing the Kingdom of Heaven, he portrays himself in this role: "Blessed are those servants whom the Master finds awake when he comes: truly, I say to you, he will [put on an apron] and have them sit at table and he will come and serve them" (Lk. 12:37).

The Prophetic Role

The Magisterium represents Jesus, who by means of his word generates the Church and gathers it in unity. The Church would have no beginning without the word; that is, the whole marvelous work of evangelization, through which the ministers of the Church cause the Word of God — which is a presence of God — to rain down upon the whole earth. Naturally, as Sesboue says, "The Church cannot be content with simply transmitting the words of Scripture; it must in turn speak. . . .

The Magisterium guarantees the orderliness of this whole expression of the faith, and is the place where its authenticity is discerned." [19]

Emile Mersch, in considering the infallibility of the pope and of the bishops, reaches the point of making the following statement with regard to the prophetic function of the hierarchy:

A sort of "Real Presence" is found in the pope and the episcopate. The Son of man is sure enough of His mystical undertaking in our race to give us His pledge that He would reside in the pope and the bishops until the end of the centuries, and that their shortcomings in knowledge would not keep Him from being the truth in them. . . . [20]

The Priestly Role

Jesus is the one and eternal Priest of the new covenant. Every priestly function, therefore, will have to be a participation in the one priesthood of Jesus. Such a reality is present in the priestly people, the Church. This is the "royal priesthood" of the faithful. In the life of its members, the

Church, Christ's Body, continues to offer itself — Christ — to the Father for the world. The priest helps the People of God to live their priestly reality; and to unite their offering of themselves in the Eucharistic assembly, to the one, true sacrifice of Christ.

In addition, the minister represents Jesus the Priest in a special way. During the Mass, Christ is present in him in the strict sense of the word; the priest visibly represents the invisible Christ. And there the priest reveals all his dignity, all the glory with which Jesus has clothed him.

In speaking of the "priest" I am speaking of one who has the fullness of the priesthood; that is, the bishop.

Mediation

Jesus is also the only Mediator between God and the human race. The hierarchy is not a mediator, but it is the sacrament (the visible sign) of the one Mediator, Jesus. The bishops manifest Jesus the Mediator.

In the divine plan all things must come to pass through the action of human beings. The Father would have had thousands of ways to save the human race, but he accomplished the work of salvation through a man: the Word Incarnate. And Jesus likewise uses human beings, as we have been able to verify through our study of the hierarchy. And even when it seems that God is acting directly, as when he adorns his Church with charisms, he does not recognize the actions of the persons to whom — for the benefit of humanity — he has given these gifts, if they do not first pass through the scrutiny of his ministers.

And finally, Therese of Lisieux states that:

His creatures are all at his service and he — Jesus — loves to make use of them during the night of life in order to conceal his adorable presense. Nevertheless, he does not conceal himself to such an extent that we cannot catch sight of him. [21]

6.

Collegial Communion

Communion Between the Churches

In a previous chapter we spoke about the individual bishops. Now we are going to speak about the rapport between the bishops. Let us listen to these words spoken by Paul VI during his homily at an episcopal consecration:

Who are the friends of a bishop? . . . The first category is that of the bishops themselves . . . to whom, in the person of the apostles, the New Commandment to love one another was given first and foremost. . . . The second category is that composed of the whole human race.[1]

The ecumenical document of the Group of Dombes, *The Episcopal Ministry,* states:

The New Testament makes reference to fraternal visits which they [the shepherds] make to one another (Acts 21:17-18; Gal. 2:1-10), to exchanges of letters (Col. 4:16), to the sending of ministers to new communities (Acts

11:19-26; 13:1-3), to collections taken up for the churches in difficulty (2 Cor. 8:9), and to gatherings which allow them to make common decisions (Acts 15:1-35). This network of relationships, which reveals the birth of a body of ministers, expresses the unity among the individual churches within the universal Church.[2]

In the third century Cyprian recommended unity among the bishops in these words:

> This unity is what we must firmly conserve and defend; we bishops above all . . . so that we will be able to prove that the episcopate is also one and undivided . . . There is one episcopate and each one for his part possesses it entirely.[3]

And Basil, writing to Atarbius, Bishop of Neocaesarea, also urges unity among the churches:

> . . . If we on the side of the Church do not wage a battle equal to that conducted by the adversaries of sound doctrine . . . nothing will be able to prevent the truth from perishing . . . and ourselves from also participating in its condemnation, through not having shown . . . the concern for the unity of the churches which should be expected of us.[4]

Irenaeus, in his famous letter to Pope Victor, informs us that at that time, the bishops used to send the Eucharist to one another as a sign of communion.

The Apostolic College and the Episcopal College

The unity of the apostolic body is also exemplified in the episcopal college. The episcopal consecration brings about an ontological transformation in one's being, so that the bishops are one with one another precisely because of this consecration. The theologian Anciaux says: "An ontological and sacramental unity exists among the bishops because it was expressly desired and instituted by Jesus."[5]

The historian Maccarrone affirms that already at the beginning of the second century, Ignatius of Antioch considered Christ to be the operative and dynamic cause of the unity of the bishops. It is Christ who makes them one.

[This Father of the Church] is the first to clearly formulate the doctrine of the unity and the uniqueness of the episcopate . . . by virtue of an immanent action [that is, which works from within] of Christ, which unites the bishops, bringing about in them [through their consecration] a convergence of doctrine about himself [Christ] and . . . the union of each one in Christ, which makes of the bishops dispersed throughout the world a perfect unity.[6]

This is wonderful! All the bishops are one because in all of them it is Christ who acts. Therefore, Christ is present in them in a very special way, and he makes them one among themselves. But let us listen to the words of Ignatius:

I have taken the initiative to exhort you to be in accord with the mind of God. For Jesus Christ, our inseparable life, is the mind of the Father . . . even as the bishops, appointed throughout the world are in the mind of Christ.[7]

The bishops are one among themselves because they are all one with the mind of Christ. To all of them, Christ gives his mind, his Truth — which is he himself. And for this reason they are one.

The uniqueness of the episcopate signifies that

there is only one episcopal office: that of Christ. And Christ shares this with the bishops. As Cyprian says: "Just as there is only one Church spread throughout the whole world in many members, so there is only one episcopate represented by a multiplicity of bishops united among themselves."[8]

The bishop, therefore, is part of an episcopal body, and only in unity with the whole body — which the Second Vatican Council calls the "College," can he carry out his role well.

Collegiality and Vatican II

The Second Vatican Council clearly refers back to the patterns of Church life in the second and third centuries for the doctrinal content of the word "college." For as we have already mentioned, during those centuries the bishops were strongly aware of their duty to strive to be of one mind regarding the facts of the apostolic and ecclesiastical tradition; of their obligation to maintain communion with one another through the exchange of letters of peace, or through decisions made together at various levels (local, regional and interregional); and of the need to maintain communion with the bishop of Rome.

The life of the college of bishops in the first centuries is an expression of their *communio,* a reality at once mystical and juridical. In fact, the bishops either acted collegially in the strict sense of the word, as in the case of provincial and regional councils; or they acted on the basis of mutual understandings, involving reciprocal consultations, exchanges of letters of peace, and so on. But in all cases they acted in *communio.*[9]

The concept of episcopal collegiality has emerged from the Second Vatican Council with a precise and complete theological content.[10] The Council states that Jesus established the twelve apostles "after the manner of a college or a fixed group over which he placed Peter, chosen from among them."[11] And it continues:

Just as the role that the Lord gave individually to Peter, the first among the apostles, is permanent and was meant to be transmitted to his successors, so also the apostles' office of nurturing the Church is permanent, and was meant to be exercised without interruption by the sacred order of bishops.[12]

Just as, by the Lord's will, St. Peter and the other apostles constituted one apostolic college, so in a similar way the Roman Pontiff as the successor of Peter, and the bishops as the successors of the apostles are joined together.[13]

... [Each new bishop] is constituted a member [of the college] by virtue of sacramental consecration and by hierarchical communion with the head and members of the body.[14]

In the Prefatory Note to the third chapter of *Lumen Gentium,* the Constitution on the Church, we read that the word *"College* is not understood in a *strictly juridical* sense, namely, of a group of equals who entrust their power to their president, but of a stable group whose structure and authority is to be deduced from revelation."[15] The Council does not go into an explanation of the possible structure of the college, but it affirms that this explanation is to be found in revelation.

The Prefatory Note continues: "While the College always exists, it does not for that reason permanently operate through *strictly* collegial action. . . ."[16] It always exists as a college but it does not always act as such.

The Effects of Episcopal Consecration

In the words of the Council, "episcopal consecration, together with the office of sanctifying, also confers the offices of teaching and of governing."[17] Therefore, three offices are conferred. The Council states that all three offices originate directly from the sacrament, and this is because all together they constitute the fullness of the sacrament of Orders. This is, indeed, an enhanced vision of the sacramental nature of the episcopate.

When a bishop has received a "canonical mission"; that is, when a particular territory and its people have been assigned to his care, he may then freely exercise his offices. The Council has re-emphasized the ancient conception of the Church, according to which the three offices are conferred by the sacrament, but the exercise of these faculties is given with the assignment of a canonical mission.[18]

The Supreme Power in the Church

With regard to the supreme power in the Church, the Council states:

. . . the college or body of bishops has no authority unless it is simultaneously conceived of in terms of its head, the Roman Pontiff . . . and without any lessening of his power of primacy over all, pastors as well as the general faithful. For in virtue of his office, that is, as Vicar of Christ and Pastor of the Whole Church, the Roman Pontiff has full, supreme, and universal power over the Church. And he can always exercise this power freely.

The order of bishops . . . together with its head . . . is the subject of supreme and full power over the universal Church. But this power can be exercised only with the consent of the Roman Pontiff.[19]

In the Church then, by divine right, we find the supreme power of the pope, and the supreme power of the college together with its head. The Council continues:

For Our Lord made Simon Peter alone the rock and key-bearer of the Church (cf. Mt. 16:18-19), and appointed him shepherd of the whole flock (cf. Jn. 21:15ff.)

It is definite, however, that the power of

binding and loosing, which was given to Peter (Mt. 16:19), was granted also to the college of apostles, joined with their head (Mt. 18:18; 28:16-20). This college, insofar as it is composed of many, expresses the variety and universality of the People of God, but insofar as it is assembled under one head, it expresses the unity of the flock of Christ. In it [the college], the bishops . . . recognizing the primacy . . . of their head, exercize their own authority for the good of their own faithful, and indeed of the whole Church, with the Holy Spirit constantly strengthening its organic structure and inner harmony.

The supreme authority with which this college is empowered over the whole Church is exercised in a solemn way through an ecumenical council. . . . The same collegiate power can be exercised . . . by the bishops living in all parts of the world, provided that the head of the college calls them to collegiate action, or at least so approves or freely accepts the united action of the dispersed bishops, that it is made a true collegiate act. [20]

There are, therefore, various ways through

which the college can participate in the exercise of this supreme power: in the councils; when the pope explicitly invites the bishops to express themselves; or when he approves or accepts their common actions.

But there is a whole spectrum of ways in which this collegiality is lived out. So that whatever an individual bishop or a group of bishops gathered in council decides with regard to the life of faith in their local churches, in the light of their particular social context; as well as whatever the various bishops report on in their normal relations with the Holy See — all have an influence on the universal Church.

The pope has the right to decide at his own discretion whether to act personally or collegially. [21]

The Authority of the Pope

According to the Catholic Church, the pope is the Vicar of Christ in the exercise of his authority, and he is the visible head of the Church. As such, he is distinct from all other Christians, bishops and faithful alike. His primacy is not only a primacy of honor or supervision, but of jurisdiction. The pope has the *munus;* that is, the commission or the mandate to shepherd the universal Church. He has immediate authority over all members of the Church, without need of any intermediary, and his authority is full and universal.

The Authority of the Bishops

The authority of the individual bishops is not full, in that its exercise depends upon the pope. However, with respect to the faithful of his own diocese, each bishop possesses true episcopal authority, which is both ordinary and immediate. In their regard, he has authority as the vicar of Christ. And we find the following statement in *Lumen Gentium* about the bishops:

Their power, therefore, is not destroyed by the supreme and universal power [of the pope]. On the contrary it is affirmed, strengthened, and vindicated thereby, since the Holy Spirit unfailingly preserves the form of government established by Christ the Lord in his Church. [22]

Each of the individual bishops in the Church

over which he is placed must carry out the exercise of his office in harmony with the head and members of the college, thereby ensuring that he is a living expression of the permanent college that Christ intended.

Every bishop has the same mission as the original apostles: the preaching of the Gospel to "all nations" (Mt. 28:19). Therefore "episcopal preaching is inherently universal." [23]

The Infallibility of the College

The infallibility of the episcopate in communion with the pope, even though scattered throughout the world, has certainly been the doctrine of the Catholic Church. But the first Vatican Council was prevented from dogmatically defining it by the political events of the time. The Second Vatican Council has clearly defined it:

Although the individual bishops do not enjoy the prerogative of infallibility, they can nevertheless proclaim Christ's doctrine infallibly. This is so, even when they are dispersed around the world, provided that while maintaining the bond of unity among themselves and with Peter's successor, and while teaching authentically on a matter of faith or morals, they concur in a single viewpoint as the one which must be held conclusively. This authority is even more clearly verified when, gathered together in an ecumenical council, they are teachers and judges of faith and morals for the universal Church. Their definitions must then be adhered to with the submission of faith. [24]

The infallibility of the pope had already been clearly affirmed by the First Vatican Council, and the Second Vatican Council reaffirmed it.

The College, Instrument of the Unity of the Church

The pope and the bishops are the constitutional and, therefore, fundamental instrument of the unity and catholicity of the Church. They are a "charismatic" instrument — since ministry is also a gift of the Spirit — and not a "sociological" tool. As Dianich expresses it:

The college serves the unity of the whole

Church . . . whose internal unity is entrusted . . . to the relationships of communion between the episcopal college itself and its head, the successor of Peter, who is invested with the charism of being the rock of unity. [25]

Pietro Parente states that the link and the union between the college and its head do not exist only in a moral or juridical sense, but "in the supernatural sphere of the Mystical Body, which, though neither physical nor moral, is real, belonging to a superior order of reality." [26]

The pope, though head of the college, is not an outside person on whom the college depends. Without its head the college is inconceivable; it cannot exist. Paul VI expressed himself in these words in his closing address to the third session of the Council:

We do not fear that our authority is diminished or hindered as . . . we celebrate yours, but rather we feel even stronger because of the union which makes us brothers together. We feel better able to guide the universal Church, knowing that each one of you is striving for the same goal; and we feel more confident in the help of Christ because we all are and want to be more closely gathered together in his name." [27]

The bishops do not hinder the authority of the pope. They strengthen it, because together with the pope they establish the presence of Jesus in the midst of the college.

The Church and its Government as Presented by the Council

With the Second Vatican Council, the Church has taken an enormous step forward, and the proofs to demonstrate this are inexhaustible. It is enough to see how the Council presents the Church and its government. Both are shown to be in the image of God.

Jesus founded the Church in the image of God, who is one and triune. In fact, through baptism and, above all, through the Eucharist, the faithful are made one, because they are transformed into Christ and incorporated into his Mystical Body. In the Body of Christ, however, besides the unity of the body, there is also the plurality of the members.

Christ's Body, the Church, is one also because of the very special presence of Christ in the pope, which is the origin and cause of the unity among the bishops and among all the faithful. And yet there is distinction in the Church, because in the local churches there are the bishops, in whom the glorified Christ, Christ the Head, is present; and he makes every local church "Church."

The Church's government corresponds to a precise plan of God, and its operation is "mysterious." It has no parallels in human society. The way Jesus conceives the government of the Church seems to me a masterpiece of his divine genius.

What has been said about the Church can also be said about the government of the Church; even more so, since all the bishops, including the pope, are even more one among themselves than the faithful, through the episcopate, which has made them even more one with Christ.

The government of the Church can also be thought of in terms of the unity and trinity of God: the pope has supreme power; the college likewise has supreme power.

Gerard Philips writes: "The Scholastics would say that the *subiectum agens* ['the acting subject'] is at times the pope, at times the college presided over by the pope." [28]

The pope calls to mind the unity of God; the college, composed of a plurality of persons, calls to mind, by analogy, the Trinity.

When the pope governs alone, he acts as the Vicar of Christ and head of the whole Church; when he acts with the college, he acts as head of the college.

But since, even when the pope acts alone, it is Christ working in him, because of the particular grace with which the pope is invested; and since Christ is also present in the acts of the college, because, as a result of the episcopal consecration and the hierarchical communion, he lives among the bishops united together with the pope, we can say that the Church is actually governed by one Person alone: Jesus, who at times acts through the pope, and at times through the college.

Abbreviations

Abbott	Walter M. Abbott, editor. *The Documents of Vatican II.* New York, 1966.
Dombes	The Group of Dombes. *Le ministère épiscopal.* Taizé, 1976.
ECF	*Early Christian Fathers.* Cyril C. Richardson, translator, editor. New York, 1970.
Insegnamenti	*Insegnamenti di Paolo VI.* 15 Vols. to date. Vatican City, 1963 - .
NRT	*Nouvelle revue théologique.*
PG	J.P. Migne. *Patrologiae Cursus Completus, Series Graeca.* 162 Vols. Paris, 1857 - 1866.
PL	J.P. Migne. *Patrologiae Cursus Completus, Series Latina.* 221 Vols. Paris, 1844 - 1864.
TAF	*The Apostolic Fathers.* Kirsopp Lake, translator. 2 Vols. Cambridge, Mass., 1952.

The Revised Standard Version of the Bible has been used throughout, except where, for greater clarity, a direct translation (indicated by *) has been made from the Greek.

Notes

Chapter 1

1. *Ekklesia,* April 15, 1966, cited in *Insegnamenti,* IV (1966), p. 809.
2. Leo the Great, *Sermons* 4,2 (*PL* 54, 150).
3. Oscar Cullmann, cited by J. Guitton in *Dialoghi con Paolo VI* (Milan, 1967), pp. 220-221.
4. *Insegnamenti,* III (1965), pp. 1105-1106.
5. Ambrose, *Exposition on the Psalms* 40, 30 (*PL* 14. 1134).
6. John Chrysostom, *Homilies on the Gospel of Matthew* 54, 2 (*PG* 58, 534).
7. Catherine of Siena, Letter 185, in *Epistolario,* I (Alba, 1966), p. 43.
8. See Augustine, *Commentary on the Gospel of John* 6, 1 (*PL* 35, 1428).
9. John Chrysostom, *Homilies on 2 Timothy* 2, 4 (*PG* 62, 612).
10. Hilary of Poitiers, *Commentary on Matthew* 10, 4 (*PL* 9, 967).
11. Augustine, *Commentary on the Gospel of John* 50, 12 (*PL* 35, 1763).
12. Peter Chrysologus, *Sermons* 6 (*PL* 52, 202-203).
13. *Insegnamenti* III (1965), pp. 1110 - 1111.
14. Gregory of Nyssa, *Eulogy II on St. Stephen* (*PG* 46, 729, 733).

Chapter 2

1. See Gérard Philips, *L'Eglise et son mystère,* I (Paris, 1967), p. 205.
2. Gregory the Great, *Exposition on the Book of Job* XXVIII, 5 (*PL* 76, 455).
3. Augustine, *Exposition on the Psalms* 86, 4 (*PL* 37, 1103).
4. *Lumen Gentium,* Art. 19, Abbott, p. 38.
5. See G. Dejaifve, "Episcopat et college apostolique", *NRT* 85 (1963), p. 811.

6. See Philips, p. 231.
7. Gregory the Great, *Job* XXVIII, 18, 38 (*PL* 76, 470).
8. See Piet Fransen, "Orders and Ordination" in *Sacramentum Mundi: An Encyclopedia of Theology*, IV (New York, 1969), p. 308.
9. See W. Trilling, *Hausordnung Gottes* (Düsseldorf, 1960), p. 49.
10. André Lemaire, *I ministeri nella Chiesa* (Bologna, 1977), p. 29.
11. Lemaire, p. 31.
12. Tertullian, *On the Prescription against the Heretics*, 22, (*PL* 2, 34).
13. Tertullian, 21 (*PL* 2, 33).
14. Maximus of Turin, *Homilies* 41 (*PL* 57, 319 - 320).
15. L. Bouyer, *L'Eglise de Dieu* (Paris, 1970), p. 381.
16. Ambrose, *Exposition on the Gospel of Luke* 6, 59 (*PL* 15, 1802).

Chapter 3

1. John Chrysostom, *Homilies on the Epistle of Paul to the Colossians* 3, 5 (*PL* 54, 154).
2. Leo the Great, *Sermons* 5, 3 (*PL* 54, 154).
3. *Lumen Gentium*, Art. 21, Abbott, pp. 40-42.
4. Bouyer, p. 398.
5. Bouyer, p. 399.
6. Clement of Rome, *First Letter to the Corinthians* 42, 1-2, *ECF* p. 62.
7. Clement, 42, 3-4, *ECF* p. 62.
8. Irenaeus, *Against Heresies* IV, 26, 2 (*PG* 7, 1053); see also Dombes, Art. 29.
9. Tertullian, *On the Prescription against Heretics* 32 (*PL* 2, 44-45).
10. *Insegnamenti*, II (1964), p. 701.
11. Didache 11, 4, trans. F.X. Glimm in *The Fathers of the Church, Vol 1: The Apostolic Fathers*, ed. L. Schopp and others (New York, 1946), p. 180.

12. *Didache* 11, 7, Glimm, p. 180.
13. *Didache* 13, 2, Glimm, p. 182.
14. *Didache* 15, 1-2, Glimm, p.183.
15. B. Bartmann, *Teologia Dogmatica* (Alba, 1949), p. 958.
16. Ignatius of Antioch, *To the Magnesians* 3,1 (*PG* 5, 665). *TAF*, I, p. 199.
17. Dombes, Art. 11.
18. Dombes, Art. 12.
19. Ignatius, *To the Trallians* 3, 1 (*PG* 5, 677), *ECF* p. 99.
20. Ignatius, *To the Magnesians* 6, 1 (*PG* 5, 668). *TAF*, I, p. 203.
21. *To the Magnesians* 3, 2 (*PG* 5, 665), *TAF*, I, p. 199
22. Ignatius, *To the Ephesians* 1, 3 (*PG* 5, 644). *ECF*, p. 88.
23. Jerome, *Commentary on the Letter of Paul to the Ephesians* 3, 5 (*PL* 26, 563).
24. Jerome, *Letters* III, 82, 11 (*PL* 22, 742).
25. Peter Chrysologus, *Sermons* 167 (*PL* 52, 636).
26. Gregory the Great, *Exposition on the Book of Job* XXIV, 25, 5 (*PL* 76, 318).
27. Gregory the Great, *Letters* II, 23 (*PL* 77, 559).
28. Gregory the Great, *Forty Homilies on the Gospels* I, 17, 13 (*PL* 76, 1146).
29. Catherine of Siena, L101, *Il Messaggio di Santa Caterina da Siena: Dottore della Chiesa* (Rome, 1970) pp. 589-590.
30. Ignatius, *To the Ephesians* 6, 1 (*PG* 5, 649), *ECF* p. 89.
31. Ignatius, *To the Smyrnaeans* 8, 1-2 (*PG* 5, 713).
32. *To the Smyrnaeans* 9, 1 (*PG* 5, 713, 716).
33. Irenaeus, *Against Heresies* IV, 26, 2 (*PG* 7, 1053).
34. Cyprian, *Letters* 59. 5 (*PL* 3, 802).
35. John Chrysostom, *Homilies on the Letter to the Hebrews* 34, 1 (*PG* 63, 231-233).
36. Catherine of Siena, D 116, *Il Messaggio* (above, note 29), p. 121.
37. *Lumen Gentium*, Art. 20, Abbott, p. 40.
38. *L.G.*, Art. 26, Abbott, pp. 50-51.

39. *L.G.*, Art. 27, Abbott, pp. 51-52.
40. Philips (above, Ch. 2, note 1), p. 355.
41. *Insegnamenti* XII (1974), p. 867.

Chapter 4

1. Dombes, Art. 22.
2. Ignatius, *To the Romans*, preface (*PG* 5, 685).
3. Ignatius, *To the Trallians* 13, 1 (*PG* 5, 684), *TAF*, I. p. 225.
4. See Johannes Quasten, *Patrology* I (Utrecht, 1966), p. 69.
5. Quasten, p. 68.
6. Quasten, p. 70.
7. Ignatius, *To the Romans* 3, 1 (*PG* 5, 688): see also B. Bartmann (above, Ch. 3, note 15), p. 958.
8. See Ignatius, *Romans* 4, 3 (*PG* 5, 689).
9. P. Batiffol, *La Chiesa nascente e il cattolicesimo* (Florence, 1971), p. 130.
10. Clement of Rome, *First Letter to the Corinthians* 44, 3, *ECF* pp. 63-64.
11. Clement, 47, 6, *ECF*, p. 65.
12. Clement, 57, 1, *ECF*, p. 69.
13. Clement, 59, 1, *ECF*, p. 70.
14. Clement, 63, 2-3, *ECF*, p. 73.
15. Irenaeus, *Against Heresies* III, 3, 2 (*PG* 7, 848).
16. Tertullian, *On the Prescription against the Heretics* 36 (*PL* 2, 49).
17. Cyprian, *Letters* 43, 5.
18. Cyprian, *On the Unity of the Church* 4 (*PL* 4, 498-501).
19. Gregory of Nazianzen, *Carmina* 2, 1 (*PG* 37, 1068).
20. Bartmann (above, Ch. 3, note 15), p. 1023.
21. John Chrysostom, *On the Priesthood* 2, 1 (*PG* 48, 632).
22. John Chrysostom, *Homilies on the Letter of Paul to the Romans* 32, 2 (*PG* 60, 677-678).
23. Augustine, *Letters* 53, 1-2 (*PL* 33.196).

24. Augustine, *Letters* 181, 1 (*PL* 33, 780).
25. Leo the Great, *Sermons* 4, 2, (*PL* 54, 149).
26. Leo, *Sermons* 4, 3 (*PL* 54, 151-152).
27. Leo, *Sermons* 5, 4 (*PL* 54, 155).
28. Leo, *Letters* 5, 2 (*PL* 54, 615).
29. Philips (above, Ch. 2, note 1), p. 286.
30. Catherine of Siena, P 3, in *Il Messaggio* (above, Ch. 3, note 29), p. 569.
31. Catherine of Siena, D 115, in *Il Messaggio*, p. 553.
32. *Insegnamenti*, II (1964), p. 809.
33. *Insegnamenti*, II (1964), p. 703.
34. *Insegnamenti*, III (1965), p. 1110-1111.
35. Jean Guitton, *Dialoghi con Paolo VI* (Milan, 1967), p. 212.

Chapter 5

1. Ignatius, *To the Ephesians* 4, 1 (*PG* 5, 648), *ECF* p. 89.
2. *To the Ephesians* 4,2 (*PG* 5, 648), *ECF* p. 89.
3. Tertullian, *Exhortation on Chastity* 7 (*PL* 2, 971).
4. See *Insegnamenti*, XI (1973), p. 669; see also Bouyer (above, Ch. 2, note 15), pp. 373-399.
5. Chales Journet, *L'Eglise du Verbe incarné*, I (Bruges, 1962), p. 31.
6. *Insegnamenti*, II (1964), p. 980.
7. Alfredo Marranzini, "Ministero della Chiesa e ministeri nella Chiesa", *La Civiltà Cattolica*, 3018 (1976), pp. 550-551.
8. Edward D. O'Connor, "Charism and Institution", *American Ecclesiastical Review*, 168 (1974), p. 524.
9. Yves Congar, "Quelques problèmes touchant les ministères", *NRT* 93 (1971), p. 792.
10. *Insegnamenti*, III (1965), p. 642.
11. Philips (above. Ch. 2, note 15), p. 226.
12. See *Lumen Gentium*, Art. 3, Abbott, p. 16.
13. *Insegnamenti*, IV (1966), pp. 863-865.
14. See Bouyer (above, Ch. 2, note 15), p. 197.

15. See Congar, "La gerarchia come servizio secondo il N.T. e i documenti della tradizione" in *Episcopato e la Chiesa universale*, (Rome, 1965), p. 107.
16. Congar, "La gerarchia...," p. 94.
17. *Insegnamenti*, III (1965), pp. 984-985.
18. L. Laberthonnière, cited by Congar in "La gerarchia...," p. 111.
19. B. Sesboüé, "Autorité du Magistere et vie de foi ecclésiale," *NRT*, 93 (1971), p. 358.
20. Emile Mersch, *The Theology of the Mystical Body* (St. Louis, 1951), p. 525.
21. Thérèse of Lisieux, Letter 127, in *Gli* scritti (Rome, 1970), p. 597.

Chapter 6

1. *Insegnamenti*, XII (1974), p. 623.
2. Dombes, Art. 21.
3. Cyprian, *On the Unity of the Church* 5 (*PL* 4, 501).
4. Basil, *Letters* 65 (*PG* 32,421); see also *Letters* 66 (*PG* 32, 424-425).
5. Paul Anciaux, "L'épiscopat comme realité sacramentelle," *NRT*, 85 (1963), p. 158.
6. M. Maccarrone, "Apostolicita, episcopato e primato di Pietro," *Lateranum* (Rome, 1967), p. 9.
7. Ignatius, *To the Ephesians* 3, 2 (*PG* 5, 645), *ECF*, p. 88.
8. Cyprian, *Letters* 55, 24, cited in A. Donato, *L'unità della Chiesa, La preghiera del Signore*, (Rome, 1967), p. 33.
9. See G. D'Ercole, *"Communio, collegialità, primato e "sollecitudo omnium ecclesiarum" dai vangeli a Costantino,* (Rome, 1964), pp. 299-300; 312ff.
10. See B. Gherardini, *La Chiesa oggi e sempre*, (Milan, 1974), p. 163.
11. *Lumen Gentium,* Art. 19, Abbott, p. 38.
12. *L.G.*, Art. 20, Abbott, p. 40.
13. *L.G.*, Art. 22, Abbott, p. 42.

14. *L.G.*. Art. 22, Abbott, p. 43.
15. *L.G.*, Prefatory note 1, Abbott, pp. 98-99.
16. *L.G.*, Prefatory note 4, Abbott, p. 100.
17. *L.G.*, Art. 21, Abbott, p. 41.
18. See O. Robleda, *Quaestiones disputatae juridico-canonicae*, (Rome, 1969), pp. 111-117, 123-128; see also Robleda in *Periodica*, 59 (1970), pp. 670-671, 676-677.
19. *L.G.* Art. 22, Abbott, p. 43.
20. *L.G.* Art. 22, Abbott, pp. 43-44.
21. See *L.G.*, Prefatory Note 3, Abbott, p. 100.
22. *L.G.*, Art. 27, Abbott, p. 52.
23. U. Betti, "Magistero episcopale e magistero pontificio nel Vaticano II," in *L'ecclesiologia dal Vaticano I al Vaticano II* (Brescia, 1973), p. 204.
24. *L.G.*, Art. 25, Abbott, p. 48.
25. S. Dianich, *La Chiesa mistero di comunione* (Turin, 1975), p. 155.
26. Pietro Parente, *Teologia di Cristo*, II (Rome, 1971), p. 261, n. 80.
27. *Insegnamenti* II (1964), p. 670.
28. Philips (above, Ch. 2, note 1), p. 259.

COLLECTION OF THE WORKS OF CHIARA LUBICH

The Eucharist

This work, in a contemporary approach, brings together much of the wisdom of the Church. The Eucharist comes across here as a prolongation of Christ's incarnation through the centuries, a possibility for everyone to form "one body" with Christ and with all men.

93 pp. ISBN 0-911782-30-3   Paper $1.95

"Jesus In the Midst"

In this collection of talks the author examines the spiritual presence of Christ in the community. The treatment of the topic rests on a most authentic tradition of the Church, reaching back to the Church Fathers. It is not just an out-growth of speculative thought, however, but the fruit of a genuine Christian experience based on Scripture. This is what makes it convincing, timely, and attractive for the Christian today.

80 pp. ISBN 0-911782-26-5   Paper $1.50

The Word of Life

This book is a concise and straightforward presentation of how to live the "word of life," that is to say, the Gospel. It contains four brief talks given by Chiara Lubich to the members of the Focolare Movement. For those who look to the Gospel as the foundation for radical change, these pages are packed with new ideas for action.

95 pp. ISBN 0-911782-25-7   Paper $1.15

When Our Love is Charity

In this book Chiara Lubich deals in particular with going to God through our brother and being of one heart and of one mind in a pluralistic society. Something new, showing the inexhaustible resources of the Holy Spirit.

82 pp. 2nd printing ISBN 0-911782-24-9   Paper $1.15

That All Men Be One

This is the inspiring account of the events which surround the birth of the Focolare Movement, and the vast results that they have produced. Taking a stand against the hatred and absurdity of the second world war, putting in the balance their very lives, a small group of young girls rediscovered the truth of the Gospel with effects that were to motivate hundreds of thousands of people around the world to work for the solidarity of the human race.

105 pp. 4th printing ISBN 0-911782-21-4   Paper $1.95

Meditations

This book is a collection of meditations. Even though they originally came to life on different days and even over different years, Chiara Lubich's individual insights are linked together by one basic theme: God is Love.

148 pp. 2nd printing ISBN 0-911782-20-6   Paper $1.50

A Little 'Harmless' Manifesto

In this powerful essay Chiara Lubich expresses some of the ideas which are at the core of the spirituality of the Focolare Movement.

52 pp. ISBN 0-911782-17-6   Paper $0.95

It's A Whole New Scene

High-powered, brief thoughts for youth attracted by Jesus Christ. The book can set a fast pace in one's growth toward God and people.

67 pp. ISBN 0-911782-01-X   paper $0.75

CASSETTES

FM-1 Contemplation in the 20th Century:
      Meditations
      Part I
      $4.50 plus 50¢ shipping charges

FM-2 Contemplation in the 20th Century:
      Meditations
      Part II
      $4.50 plus 50¢ shipping charges

FM-3 God is Love
      $5.00 plus 50¢ shipping charges

FM-4 The Word of God
      $4.50 plus 50¢ shipping charges

The last two are talks of the Foundress of the Focolare Movement to the members of the Gen Movement. "New Generation," which appeals to both young and adults.

OTHER BOOKS PUBLISHED
BY NEW CITY PRESS

Focolare: After 30 Years

Sergius C. Lorit & Nuzzo M. Grimaldi

This book is an attempt to provide some information about the Focolare Movement. It is not intended to give a complete view of the subject. For the Focolare Movement, as a movement of renewal, is continually growing, expanding and developing, albeit from the strong and solid spirituality which lies at its heart.

The book contains interviews with a number of people with responsibility in the Movement at an international level, beginning with Chiara Lubich, the foundress and president. It also describes some of the activities of the Movement throughout the world.

268 pp., 136 illustrations ISBN 0-911782-27-3   Paper $4.50

Reaching for More

Pascal Foresi

The chapters in this book treat various Gospel passages in all their unsettling and fascinating reality. The author's style is informal because the book is a collection of "conversations" he had with his friends (the Focolarini). The biblical foundation is as solid as it is helpful. The author draws conclusions that can enlighten the intellect and warm the heart. This is indeed a book for modern times. It is sure to have an impact on those Christians who want to be authentic without compromise.

Fr. Foresi is the author of several theological and spiritual publications. He has contributed to the birth and development of the "Focolare" Movement. He did his philosophical and theological studies at the Gregorian and Lateran Universities in Rome. He is the head of the Department of Theological Research at the International Institute for the Apostolate of the Laity (Loppiano, Florence, Italy).

208 pp. ISBN 911782-04-4   Paper $1.50

Celibacy Put to the Gospel Test

Pascal Foresi

The title describes the content. The subject is one many responsible Christians will want to ponder. At last someone dares to cover this topic in a way that can be understood by the layman as well as the religious.

34 pp. ISBN 911782-16-8   Paper $0.50

The Gospel in Action

C. Miner

These are true stories. We see a mother, an office worker, a doctor, and others, living and working in circumstances similar to our own. Their deceptively modest experiences under normal working conditions, demonstrate the possibility of relationships among men which are humanly warm and complete but also somehow divine.

153 pp. ISBN 911782-23-0   Paper $1.50

Me Too, Forever

C. Miner

These experiences have been written down from first-hand accounts. It is typical of young people to believe in an ideal totally and to dedicate themselves to it completely. The ideal that is revealed in each of these stories is truly worthy of an absolute response, because the Ideal is God Himself.

119 pp. ISBN 911782-22-2   Paper $1.50

My Child and God
(Religious Education in the Family)

by Annemarie Zanzucchi

The method of religious education explored in this book is rooted in reality, in the experience of the author and a group of parents whom she interviews. They speak honestly and freely about the difficulty and the success they have encountered in introducing their children to God, to prayer, to Jesus and Mary, to the Scriptures, the examination of conscience, the sacraments, suffering, and death. The goal of this method is to contribute to the formation of a human being who believes in the love of God and who has learned to love.

ISBN 0-911782-31-1   Paper $2.25

Sketches of the Universe

Piero Pasolini

In this book the reader is drawn by the author into the infinitesimal world of the atom at the very heart of matter, until he reaches the point where matter itself seems to be swallowed up in abysmal nothingness and events take place in billionths of a second. Then he is led toward the ultimate expression of material creation—to man, who himself material, by a marvelous process shares in the realm of the spiritual.

This readable, swift-moving, yet rigorously scientific book will provide readers, whether or not they are qualified in this field, with enjoyment and thought-provoking inspiration.

Piero Pasolini is a physicist who has published in six languages many articles and books on the philosophical implications of scientific discovery.

248 pp. ISBN 911782-15-x   Paper $1.95

175

Everybody's Pope: John XXIII

Sergius C. Lorit

The story of the Pope who taught the world how to smile again. The author recounts the Pope's life in a popular style while not diminishing his immense moral and religious stature. A book to acquaint oneself with or keep warm the memory of this man who left so deep a mark on contemporary history.

230 pp. ISBN 911782-06-0 Paper $1.00

Charles de Foucauld: the Silent Witness

Sergius C. Lorit

Few today have not heard of the once flamboyant French officer who became the poorest among the poor in the heart of the Sahara to be closer to Christ. An intriguing biography that promises the reader light for his personal life.

174 pp. ISBN 0-911782-29-x Paper $2.50

The Last Writings of Reginald Garrigou-Lagrange

The book is a serious guide for all those who want to develop themselves in the spiritual life. Garrigou-Lagrange was a master, an expert in directing people. These are his precious last writings summarizing his outstanding career as a man who knew men.

224 pp. ISBN 911782-12-5 Cloth $5.95